Austin, Texas   Jan ~ 8 1688

Presented to Dr. J

Canthinis Come

DATE DUE

			PRINTED IN U.S.A.

CHRISTIAN FAITH VERSUS UNBELIEF

ISBN: 0-9618383-0-2
Library of Congress Catalog Number: 87-8825505

Printed by Papyrus Book Printers 21 County Rd. Chatham Il 62629

To Alice

Teammate and Friend

CONTENTS

PREFACE

This book is primarily intended for Christians. It seeks to do two things: (1) to state the nature and the reasonableness of Christian faith, and (2) to respond to some specific assertions and arguments of some unbelievers on selected topics.

In the twenty centuries of Christianity, unbelievers have written very much in opposition to Christian belief. In this book only few topics are discussed and only a limited selection of assertions and arguments of unbelievers are taken up. A thorough job of responding to the assertions and arguments of unbelievers requires many volumes.

Why dialogue with unbelievers? For one thing, the attacks against Christianity by unbelievers are there and they are being read by people. One day I was going through the card catalog of a major university. I listed a good number of titles of books on religion written by unbelievers. When I went to the shelves to look for the books, a number of them were out—which means people had borrowed them. That incident made me realize more keenly than ever that the Christian community faces the urgent task of responding to unbelievers. And if Christians do not want to admit that people are reading the writings of atheists and agnostics, they are helping the cause of unbelief. If Christians remain silent about the assertions and arguments of unbelievers, the uncommitted might think that the Christian's silence is due to the fact that indeed the unbelievers are right. A dialogue with unbelief at least makes the Christian aware of the opposing ideas and such awareness might stimulate him to weigh things for himself. It is healthy for one's Christian convictions to be tried by the fire of unbelief.

In Chapter One ("Some Preliminary Matters") I discuss some topics that I hope will serve as a useful preparation for the coming chapters. In this preliminary chapter I give expression to my deepening conviction that central to the disagreement between Christians and unbelievers are issues having to do with theory of meaning and knowledge—issues of methodology and criteria. All other issues are derivative, secondary.

In Chapter Two ("Science and Christian Faith") we consider the basic issue in the area of the relationship between science and Christian faith. Here we dialogue directly with unbelievers.

Chapter Three ("Miracles") continues the direct dialogue with unbelievers; the subject is the possibility of miracles.

In Chapters Four, Five, and Six we get more into the Christian area. Chapter Four ("God") discusses the reasonableness of belief in God.

Chapter Five ("Christian Faith") deals with the nature and the logic of Christian faith. Chapter Six ("The Bible"), the longest chapter, discusses the trustworthiness of the Bible and the Bible's place in the Christian religion.

The Bible quotations are from the Revised Standard Version.

My wife, Alice, read the entire manuscript and penciled places where changes were in order. Of course I am solely responsible for all remaining inadequacies.

Gratitude is hereby expressed to the following publishers/copyright owners for permission to use the material indicated: Faber & Faber Ltd., for material from C. Joad, The Recovery of Belief; Allen & Unwin Ltd., for material from A. Wolf's Essentials of Scientific Method; Bethany House Publishers, for material from God's Inerrant Word, ed. John W. Montgomery; Christianity Today, for sentences from a news item; William B. Eerdmans Pub. Co., for material from the following sources: The International Standard Bible Encyclopedia, ed. G. W. Bromiley; Second Thoughts on the Dead Sea Scrolls, by F. F. Bruce; Are the New Testament Documents Reliable?, by F. F. Bruce; Interpreting the Bible, by A. Berkeley Mickelsen; J. B. Lippincott Co., for material from Ecclesiastical History, by Eusebius; Prometheus Books, for material from The Encyclopedia of Unbelief, ed. Gordon Stein: Zondervan Bible Publishers, for material from the New International Version of the Bible. The Scripture quotations contained herein are from the Revised Standard Version Bible, copyright 1946, 1952, 1971 by the Division of Christian Education of the National Council of the Churches of Christ in the U.S. A., and are used by permission.

CHAPTER ZERO

MY FINDING THE WAY

In the earlier part of my spiritual journey questions played a central role. I grew up in a very religious Roman Catholic home. My mother, whom I loved and highly respected and the memory of whose piety I will always cherish, brought us up in a very religious environment. I recall that even the youngest of us had to take part in the daily evening and dawn devotional times.

When I was a teenager I began to ask questions about religious beliefs and practices. And as the War years gave me plenty of time to think, the questions that bothered me increased.

The end of the War found me back in high school. When I finished high school I got a scholarship at a Protestant university. I hoped that my questions on religion would get answered. But they were not. My real spiritual need was not met. For example, no one talked to me about being saved. Somehow, Bible became just another course. For one thing Bible grades were included in computing the grade point average. And I had to maintain a certain GPA in order to keep my scholarship.

During my undergraduate days I still went to church although not regularly. I saw more and more things in the church that bothered me. My interest in going to church was steadily eroded. Simultaneously, I was putting more and more emphasis on reasoning things out.

I finished the bachelor's degree at age 26 1/2. At that point

I had lost much of my interest in going to church. But I had not completely given up on the church. One Good Friday I attended services at three churches belonging to three denominations. The outcome of that experience was that I became even less interested in going to church. What made matters worse was that I now began to take pride in calling myself a freethinker. I became argumentative about religious matters. I made it a requirement that my reason must be satisfied before I commit myself to any religious beliefs or practices. I started to look down on religious people.

After graduation I got a job and studied part-time in graduate school. As far as my attitude towards religion was concerned, I was more and more satisfied with my freethinker stance. I finished the M.A. in English when I was 31.

Then something happened: someone gave me a red-covered complete RSV Bible as a gift. That gift proved to be the turning point of my religious quest. I said to myself, "Here I am, very argumentative about religion. But I really have not read this book for its own sake." I felt challenged to read it for what it had to say. But in my reading I made sure that no one helped me to understand it. I read that Bible very seriously by myself.

As I read, one by one my questions and objections fell down. There was no one to argue with; there was only the Bible. As I read I gradually grasped the central truth, namely, that God sent His Son Jesus Christ to die for the sins of men, and that because of the death of Christ eternal life is now available as a gift to those who own their sins to God and put their faith in Jesus Christ. After one year of reading the Bible, I made the most important decision of my life: I acknowledged my sinfulness to God and received Jesus Christ into my life as my personal Savior and Lord. I made that decision alone.

Looking back, having studied the Scriptures some more, I now see that the Holy Spirit must have been there all along as I read the Bible, opening my rebellious mind to see the truth about God and man's relation to God. The Holy Spirit must have been there ministering to my need for salvation.

At age 32, when I was only a babe in the Christian faith, I started my studies in philosophy.

As I went on in my philosophy studies I found that very much of contemporary philosophy is either agnostic or atheistic. Not all my professors were unbelievers, but the majority were. For example, in a graduate course in philosophy of religion (of all things!) our atheist professor was so ardently anti-Christian that one day he said in class that the best thing that can be done to Christians is to kill them off. He said it seriously.

Another atheist professor held the firm view that when Descartes speaks of God he is talking about nature—not about the God that Christians believe in. His interpretation showed how far one's atheist commitment influences even one's reading of texts. Any one who reads Descartes with an open mind just cannot fail to see that Descartes refers in his writings to the God that Christians believe in. And it is understandable that Descartes would be talking about the God of the Christian church. "The Cartesian philosophy springs, generally speaking, from two sources. On the one hand, Descartes received at the hands of the Jesuits a thorough training in Scholastic logic and metaphysics. . . ."[1]

The decades I spent full-time in philosophy exposed me directly to a lot of atheist and agnostic ideas. But God has kept my faith growing. For my doctoral dissertation I chose to tackle an atheist philosopher. My dissertation was a point-by-point reply to the anti-Christianity assertions and arguments of Antony Flew, an English analytic philosopher who has written much not only in pure philosophy but also in philosophical theology. At the time I wrote my dissertation Flew had already published two books and a number of journal articles attacking Christian beliefs.

I wrote this book in the hope that it would in a small way be of some help to Christians. Having passed through years of questioning and loss of interest in religion, and having been directly exposed to the ideas of atheists and agnostics, I hope to help the Christian see that he does not have to feel apologetic about his Christian faith because it is a reasonable faith;

it is in fact far more reasonable than the position of the atheist or the agnostic.

I also hope that this book will be of some help to those who are seeking but who as yet have not chosen the set of beliefs and practices to which they can commit themselves.

I even hope that the responses given in this book to the assertions and arguments of unbelievers will help to at least open the minds of those who as yet cannot see why some people are followers of Jesus Christ.

To those who are still questing, this book is an invitation to read the Bible with an open mind and to consider Jesus Christ seriously. The Spirit of God will help the unbeliever see the urgency of coming to terms with Him who gave His life on the Cross to make possible forgiveness of sins and the gift of eternal life even for the worst of sinners.

To the Christian this book is offered as a stimulus for thinking through the faith, that he may gain further confidence in the reasonableness of his Christian convictions. It is my hope that this book will help the believer fulfill the injunction of the apostle Peter to "always be prepared to make a defense to any one who calls you to account for the hope that is in you."

CHAPTER ONE

SOME PRELIMINARY MATTERS

1.1. WHY THIS BOOK?

The main reason for writing this book is that in our time there is one phenomenon that Christians cannot afford to ignore: unbelief. Atheism, agnosticism, skepticism—they are as real as the chair you are sitting on. Many unbelievers are zealous in the propagation of their views. In his biography of the atheist Joseph Lewis, Arthur Howland informs us that when Lewis was a younger man, he went into the mail order business with a capital of $62.50. Writes Howland: "Particularly did he want to circulate 'The Age of Reason.' Howland quotes Lewis as saying, 'If I can sell fifty thousand copies of that book, my life will have been worth while.' Continues Howland: "At first he was the entire staff of the business—office boy, stenographer, clerk and manager. He packed up the parcels, carried them to the post office, licked the stamps, and all the rest."[1] Lewis was then working on his first book. Joseph Lewis later became president of Freethinkers of America. He has been very active in propagating and defending his atheist views.

Now if atheists and other unbelievers are zealous in propagating and defending their convictions, Christians can do no less. We believe that what the Bible says is God's word. We believe that the truth is on our side. If we really believe that, then we must all be busy communicating and defending the teachings of the Bible.

There are Christians who think that unbelievers are unbelievers because they are covering up sins. I think this view is counter productive. There may be some atheists and agnostics and other unbelievers who are unbelievers because they are covering up sins. But there certainly are many unbelievers who are unbelievers because of intellectual considerations. Many educated atheists and agnostics are unbelievers because they adhere to certain criteria or methodologies or theories. Communists are unbelievers because they subscribe to certain political/economic and metaphysical theories. Others are unbelievers because they believe in science and they believe that science and religion are incompatible. And possibly there are unbelievers who are unbelievers for no clearly understood reasons. The trouble with thinking that unbelievers are unbelievers because they are covering up sins is that we then do not do anything about the intellectual objections that unbelievers sincerely hold. Also, our saying that unbelievers are unbelievers because they are covering up sins might turn off unbelievers who have serious objections; those people might get the idea that Christians assume that they (the unbelievers) are not intellectually honest persons. It is a better strategy to assume that unbelievers are unbelievers either because they have not yet been confronted with the Gospel or because they have some serious intellectual objections. It is conducive to dialogue to assume that the unbeliever is intellectually honest, serious, and sincere. As we work to communicate the Gospel to unbelievers, it would be helpful to address their objections directly. It is true that God's power of salvation is the Gospel (Romans 1:16). But it is also true that some people who are unbelievers on account of certain ideas they hold might be persuaded to consider the Gospel after their intellectual objections have been dealt with.

Unbelief has always been there since the birth of Christianity. But it seems that in the 20th century unbelief has become more pronounced than in earlier centuries. Why has unbelief become more pronounced in our time? There must be many reasons. One possible reason must be the impressive advances of science and technology and the belief that science and Christian faith are incompatible. Another possible reason is the loosening of inhibitions in our time. For example, there was a time when people would not admit even to friends that they were homosexual, but now homosexuals are very open about it. There was a time when it took very great courage for a man and a woman to live together without the benefit of marriage, but now the number of such cases is fast rising. Many people, it seems, do not like what the Bible teaches because they see that the Bible does not tolerate some of their ways. There is the upsurge of individualism. Children want to run their lives independently, and many times that means defying the standards and rejecting the values their grandparents and parents stand for. And so on and on.

In the 20th century the anti-God outlook commands a wide following in the world of the philosophers. In the first four decades of the 20th century logical empiricism swept across a number of countries with its doctrine that talk about God and other such things is meaningless. Bertrand Russell, certainly one of the great philosophers of the 20th century, published a book entitled Why I Am Not a Christian. Antony Flew, an English analytic philosopher who is still living at this writing, has as of now already published two books and a number of journal articles specifically attacking Christian theism.

It is not only philosophers who attack Christian beliefs. There are biologists, physicists, chemists, psychologists, psychiatrists, sociologists, and other intellectuals who reject Christianity.

Many of these unbelieving intellectuals are quite active in propagating their ideas. When I was working on this book, I consulted the on-line catalogue at the main library of a major university to see what that library carried by way of books written by unbelievers. The list I got was rather impressive.

In 1985 Prometheus Books, Buffalo, New York, published the two-volume Encyclopedia of Unbelief, edited by Dr. Gordon Stein. The large volumes of this encyclopedia contain writings of people who have rejected Christian belief.

Appendix 5 of this encyclopedia is a long list of "magazines and newspapers whose 'primary' purpose was to further religious unbelief" (p.778). The list, which purports to include magazines and newspapers published in different countries all over the world, includes 473 titles. Many of the magazines and newspapers were published before the 20th century. Of the 473 titles, 144 started publication in 1950 or later. Of the entire list of 473 magazines and newspapers, 75 were still publishing in 1985.

The October 4, 1985 issue of Christianity Today carried this news item (pp.27-28):

> In April [1985] a group of scholars met at the University of Michigan, Ann Arbor, ostensibly to discuss historical evidence surrounding Jesus. Free Inquiry magazine was the primary sponsor of the conference. Press material stated that 'tens of millions of people are exposed daily to exhortations about religion and the Bible' and alleged that this is causing an "undermining [of] (sic) traditional American Freedom.' To combat the influence of 'fundamentalist conservative religious believers,' it continued, 'it is necessary to question the validity of the Bible openly and publicly. Free Inquiry also announced that the Academy of Humanism, an international group of 35 scholars and scientists, had formed a Committee for the Scientific Examination of Religion (CSER). Its purpose is to 'submit religious claims to careful scientific and scholarly investigation and analysis.'

Unbelief has invaded the classrooms. Baptist Standard of March 11,1987 reported the decision handed down by US District Judge W. B. Hand in which the judge "banned 37 American history, social studies and home economics textbooks from Alabama schools on grounds they teach the religion of 'secular humanism' in violation of the First Amendment. In an 111-page opinion issued on March 4, Judge Hand of the US District Court for Southern Alabama sided with more than 600 plaintiffs in Mobile, Ala.—including parents and schoolteachers—who claimed the challenged books ignore Christianity and other faiths while teaching anti-Christian, humanistic values" (p. 3).

Why this book? Why should more books of this kind be written? I Peter 3:15 enjoins the Christian to be always prepared to defend the hope that is in him. We Christians know the truth revealed by God. We know the Word of God. And Jesus Christ has commanded us to proclaim the Gospel to the whole world. We are His ambassadors. The obligation is ours to tell the world what the Bible teaches. Now in the face of the unbelief that surrounds us, in the face of the zealousness of many unbelievers, it is ever more imperative that we who know the revealed truth respond to the assertions and arguments of unbelievers. It is ever more imperative that we be very clear as to what it is that we Christians believe and why. Part of the job of communicating the truths in Scripture is to address the objections posed by unbelievers. (In this book we will be able to address only few objections put forth by unbelievers. Unbelievers have published many books, articles and addresses attacking Christian faith. Many books need to be written responding to unbelief.)

If we Christians choose to be deaf and blind to the attacks launched by atheists and agnostics, we might one day be confronted by such numbers of unbelievers that we will have to reckon with their presence. It does not help any to pacify ourselves by saying we have the truth on our side. The unbelievers are busy propagating their own beliefs. They are busy trying to discredit Christianity. They are busy trying to win converts to unbelief. Shall we by our silence let the uncommitted think that ours is the wrong side?

A second reason for writing this book is that there are people who are sincerely seeking truth. There are persons who sincerely want to know what Christians believe and why. Part of the task of "preaching the Gospel to the whole creation" takes the form of answering questions about or objections to Christian faith. There is always the need to make clear to those who care to know the nature and the logic of Christian belief.

There is another reason for writing this book. We humans have been created by God intelligent. Since God created man with the ability to think, to reason, He must mean us to use this power. Now since our relationship to God is the most important aspect of our lives as Christians, we should diligently apply our intelligence to this area. We ought to endeavor to understand our faith as far as possible. We should try to see how the Bible's ideas relate to the things we deal with day by day and to the ideas we encounter in our conversation and in our reading. Understanding our faith and responding to unbeliever's objections strengthen our religious convictions and deepen our commitment to Christ.

1.2. RESPONDING TO UNBELIEVERS' ATTACKS

Whether we like it or not, we will in one way or another encounter the ideas of unbelievers. We are confronted by the attacks of unbelievers either in writing or orally. The only way we can avoid unbelievers' ideas is to close our ears and eyes to what is happening all around us. But we don't like that isolationist mentality. You don't enjoy the so-called bliss of ignorance, do you? So we might as well face the music and make preparations.

I want to say a word about the writings of atheists and other unbelievers. From one point of view, we can classify the writings of unbelievers into two classes: one class is composed of those writings which are carefully argued, carefully laid out. In replying to an unbeliever who argues his case, the first task is to determine the unbeliever's assumptions. (More is said about the significance of assumptions below, at 1.3). After we have ascertained the assumptions, then we evaluate each step of the argument.

There is a second group of writings by unbelievers. Many times you come across a book, an article or an address in which the unbeliever hurls at Christianity strongly-worded assertions. Often the assertions are just assertions; they are not supported by arguments or evidences. From my reading of the works of unbelievers, it seems that this approach is often used.

Let us look at two examples. On August 12, 1957, Joseph Lewis, president of Freethinkers of America, was interviewed over WXYZ-TV (American Broadcasting Co), in Detroit, Michigan. In response to the interviewer's question whether he would put the Koran and the sacred books of other religions in the same category as the Bible, Lewis replied: "I put them all in the same category. There's no more truth to the Koran than there is to the Bible, and I object to them being referred to as sacred writings. There is nothing sacred about them. When they are offered as divinely inspired, they are frauds."[2]

Our second example comes from the pen of Robert Ingersoll, whom some consider to be the greatest unbeliever in the United States in the nineteenth century. Speaking of prophets, apostles and other religious leaders, Ingersoll wrote:[3]

> They are devout and useless. They do not cultivate the soil. They produce nothing. They live on the labor of others. They are pious and parasitic. They pray for others, if the others will work for them. They claim to have been selected by the Infinite to instruct and govern mankind. They are 'meek' and arrogant, 'long-suffering' and revengeful.
>
> They ever have been, now are, and always will be the enemies of liberty, of investigation and science. They are believers in the supernatural, the miraculous and the absurd. They have filled the world with hatred, bigotry and fear. In defense of their creeds they have committed every crime and practiced every cruelty. (Emphasis mine)

Notice the strong language, the hyperbolic assertions. Look again at the last two sentences of the passage. This kind of writing is not uncommon in the works of unbelievers.

Why do some unbelievers talk that way about Christianity? Perhaps one reason is that it is easier to make unsupported assertions than to put forth assertions that are supported by arguments or evidence. Assertions unsupported by careful arguments or by evidence are rather easy to make. If one does not mind throwing big claims without the benefit of evidence or arguments, then high-sounding assertions against Christianity are not difficult to throw around.

In these examples we see the need for Christians to be alert, to raise questions about what they read or hear. There are people who are out to discredit Christianity. And some of them will advance high-sounding claims even if they actually have no serious basis for their claims. And you can be sure of one thing: whatever doctrine you point to, there are always people who take different sides on it. No matter how right you think your view is, you can safely assume that there are people who interpret things quite differently. And many of them are sincere; they really sincerely believe you are wrong. We Christians need to heed the injunction of I Peter 3:15 to be at all times prepared to make a defense for the hope that is in us.

Now when it comes to this second kind of writings by unbelievers the Christian has to be very careful, lest he feel inundated, confused, even discouraged. He must guard against being overwhelmed by the high-sounding statements. The fact is that Christianity does not have to be afraid to face up to the attacks of atheists or agnostics. The truth is on our side.

How should Christians respond to the assertions or arguments of unbelievers? They must deal with the assertions or arguments piece by piece—point by point. Each assertion or argument must be carefully examined, analyzed, evaluated against relevant data. Responsible response requires that we first try hard to understand accurately the opponent's position. We must not hurry to make our reply; we must take time to make sure that we have not misrepresented the unbeliever's position. Carefulness in presenting the opponent's view is the minimum requirement for a responsible reply. The Christian must respond responsibly—not emotionally. In responding to the assertions or arguments of unbelievers, the Christian must not stoop to tactics that are less than respectable. Arguments "directed to the man" (argumentum ad hominem) instead of to the argument should be avoided in all argumentation.

God has called Christians to do a job. We are ambassadors

of the Gospel. Our principal task is to positively and clearly communicate the truths that are in Scripture. The other part of our job is to defend the Gospel against unbelievers' attacks. And whether we are responding to unbelievers' attacks or positively communicating the message of God, we must keep in mind that the endurance of God's truths depends on God— not on us! Ours is to exercise faith. God's Word is our message; our part is to be faithful communicators of that message. As we proclaim and defend the truths of Scripture, let us not allow the noise of unbelief to drive us to despair. God is watching over His Word!

1.3. THE SIGNIFICANCE OF ASSUMPTIONS.

I want to emphasize as extremely important the role of assumptions. But first we must be clear as to what an assumption is. Webster's New Twentieth Dictionary gives several meanings of the verb "assume." Here we are concerned with only one of the meanings, namely: to assume is "to take for granted, or without proof; to suppose as a fact, as, to assume a principle in reasoning." One can confidently make the generalization that whoever speaks or writes assumes something, either a fact or a theory or a methodology or a criterion of meaning or knowledge. When a man argues, you can be sure that one or more assumptions underlie his arguments. The more sophisticated the speaker or writer, the greater role assumptions play in his speaking or writing. Because assumptions are things one takes for granted one normally does not state them in his discourse; sometimes you have to read much before you can tell what an author assumes. In fact, sometimes an author denies that he assumes a given thing when the reader believes that he does. This happens, for example, in the case of Antony Flew's attack on Christian theism. Some of those who have responded to Flew's criticism of Christianity have observed that Flew assumes the empiricist criterion of meaning and knowledge. In replying to these respondents, Flew explicitly denies that he assumes the empiricist criterion. After reading his two books and journal articles attacking Christian theism, I came to the firm conclusion that Flew does assume the empiricist criterion of meaning and knowledge.

Very often a man's assumptions remain unmentioned in his talk. But there they are, undergirding his assertions and arguments.

The more logical he is, the more consistently his assertions and arguments follow from his assumptions. When you have gotten hold of his assumptions, then you are better able to construct his thought; you can better see how his ideas relate to each other.

Our final point about assumptions is for us very important. It has to do with the relation between criteria of meaning or knowledge on the one hand and reality on the other. (In Chapter 6 we will discuss the distinction between the order of reality and the order of knowing; here we are concerned with the distinction between on the one hand reality and on the other criteria of meaning and knowledge.)

Language is man-made. Criteria of meaning pertain to language. The criteria of meaning that a writer or speaker assumes determine for him the boundaries of what is to count as meaningful. The criteria for knowledge that a person adopts determine for him what is to count as knowledge. Take the case of the empiricist criterion of meaning or knowledge. Empiricism is the view that claims to knowledge must be verifiable at least in principle by sense observation (including in observation the readings of scientific instruments). In other words, the empiricist criterion of meaning and knowledge amounts to the criterion employed in scientific investigation. If a person assumes the empiricist criterion of meaning, then if a sentence cannot be tested for truth or falsity by means of the techniques employed by science, then the sentence in question is judged meaningless. If a person assumes the empiricist criterion of knowledge, then any claim to knowledge that does not meet the empiricist standard is rejected. The empiricist has his own ways of accounting for the fact that there are millions who believe in God and do so seriously. Whatever explanation he comes up with, the end is that he rejects many words or sentences or knowledge claims made by those who believe in God, simply because words or sentences containing the word "God" are automatically rejected as meaningless. Since God is Spirit, God's reality or presence or working cannot be known without remainder by means of the empiricist methodology.

Let us quote from Alfred Ayer, a well-known 20th century empiricist philosopher. In Language, Truth and Logic, second edition, Ayer writes: ". . . a statement is verifiable and consequently meaningful, if some observation-statement can be deduced from it in conjunction with certain other premises, without being deducible from those other premises alone." [4] Notice the key role played by observation-statements. Suppose you present to Ayer a sentence about God. Let us say you tell Ayer that God answers the prayers of the faithful. Ayer asks you what observation-statements can be deduced from your statement. Ayer asks you what observations he (Ayer) can make to verify your statement. The observations must be performed by means of the techniques of science. Ayer will ask you, "What observations, what experiments can I set up to test the correctness of your claim that God answers the prayers of the faithful? What data will confirm your statement? How do I recognize those data?" The outcome will be that Ayer will dismiss your claim as meaningless: there is no way he can test your statement that God answers the prayers of the faithful. Let us quote again from Ayer's Language, Truth and Logic : "What is not so generally recognized is that there can be no way of proving that the existence of a god, such as the God of Christianity, is even probable. .... For if the existence of such a god were probable, then the proposition that he existed would be an empirical hypotheses . And in that case it would be possible to deduce from it, and other empirical hypotheses, certain experiential propositions which were not deducible from those other hypotheses alone. But in fact this not possible." [5] Since sentences about God are not verifiable in the way Ayer prescribes, therefore sentences about God are meaningless, and knowledge claims pertaining to God are rejected. Thus concludes Ayer the empiricist.

Now we pose our sixty-four dollar question. When we are talking about what there is, about reality, which comes first, criteria of meaning or knowledge, or reality? Reality, of course. Reality is logically prior to criteria of meaning or knowledge. Before there were any criteria, there already was reality. Since God created all that there is other than Himself, then God was already there before there were any human beings to formulate criteria! Not only that, but the activity of formulating criteria of meaning or knowledge—a sophisticated form of activity, to be sure—is several times removed from the primordial reality that is God or even the reality that is the universe. Indeed, it took man a long time before he acquired the sophistication needed to formulate criteria of meaning or knowledge. The pre-Socratic thinkers did not talk about criteria of meaning or knowledge. Concern for criteria is a modern phenomenon.

In science, which lies at the very bottom? Is it theory? Is it law? No. It is phenomena, it is reality. Data are logically prior to laws or theories or criteria. Before the first scientific generalization was formulated—whenever that was—there already was reality, phenomena were already occurring. There was a time (whenever it was) in the history of scientific investigation that the first generalization was formulated. And it was formulated on the basis of data. The entire architecture of science is anchored on data. That is why observation is the key ingredient in the methodology of science. Of course, when many generalizations have been formulated, these generalizations serve as guidelines to the scientist; he assumes them as he conducts his investigations. Generalizations that have been confirmed by many experiments acquire a higher rank and are dignified with the title "laws of science."

The empiricist philosopher David Hume (died 1776) gave the world a very shrewd analysis of cause and effect; his theory shows that the principle of cause and effect is dependent on data, on raw observation of phenomena. (We will discuss Hume's theory of knowledge in Chapter 3.)

The progress of science shows in a dramatic way that data

are logically prior to methodology or criteria or theory. Here is a scientist working in the laboratory. He has studied science in the university. He knows many scientific laws. Now suppose that in his experimentation he stumbles upon one datum that cannot be explained in terms of any of the scientific laws in the books. The datum is something that could not have been expected to show up in his experiments. He is puzzled. He repeats the experiment carefully; the same thing happens. Curious, the scientist performs the same experiment many times; he gets the same result, the puzzling datum continues to show up. Now such an incident could mean a discovery. It has happened many, many times in the history of science that a puzzling datum turned out to be a discovery. After enough data have been accumulated that substantiate a hypothesis that runs counter to some long-accepted generalization, then the generalization in question has to be abandoned or modified, as the case may be. A new generalization gets into the books; science has made progress. That, simply, is how science progresses. Laws are formulated on the basis of data, and laws that can no longer be squared with new data are modified or abandoned. If there is a discrepancy between received law and data, law gives way. This is what we mean by saying that data are logically prior to criteria or methodology or law. Criteria or methodology determine what can be <u>known</u>, but they cannot determine what there is. That being the case, the question of the reality of God cannot be decided merely by appealing to any criteria or methodology or theory.

The empiricist cannot <u>deny</u> the <u>reality</u> of God. Strictly speaking, the empiricist cannot be a theist or an atheist. The empiricist denies the <u>knowability</u> of God or of anything else that cannot be investigated by means of the techniques of science. The empiricist denies the <u>meaningfulness</u> of words or sentences which cannot be tested by science. And if a sentence is meaningless, then we cannot even raise the question of whether it is true, since a meaningless sentence cannot express a true proposition. The charge of being meaningless is a very radical charge. The empiricist criterion of meaningfullness renders the Bible and the books written by theologians nonsensical.

If the position of the agnostic is radical, that of the atheist is even more radical. For the atheist denies the reality of God; the atheist holds outright that there is no God. The philosopher Antony Flew holds what can be seen as an extreme form of atheism. Flew does not grant that there is a <u>concept</u> of God. Flew thinks that the agnostic grants far too much, since for Flew the agnostic grants that there is a concept of God. For Flew, the word "God" does not stand for anything, not even a concept. Flew's brand of atheism is far more radical than the kind of atheism that is widely known.

What happens if a speaker or writer <u>assumes</u> atheism? If a person assumes atheism, then of course all that the Christian holds about God and man's relation to God is not only meaningless; it is downright foolish. To the atheist all the practices of Christianity are no more than sheer foolishness. The atheist would say, "Poor Christians, how serious they are in their delusion." The atheist thinks that Christians deceive themselves when they say they worship God; there is nothing for them to worship, since there is no God.

For most if not all intellectual unbelievers, the source of atheism or agnosticism is commitment to a methodology or a criterion of meaning or knowledge. This is one reason it is very important to try to determine the assumptions that underlie a writer's or speaker's statements.

I hope I have now shown how important it is to get at a man's assumptions. When you read or listen to anyone, ask yourself what assumptions underlie what he says. If a man is logical in his thinking, then what he says follows from his assumptions. If you know a man's assumptions, you know more than half of his position. For most if not all intellectual unbelievers, the source of unbelief is commitment to a methodology or a criterion of meaning or knowledge.

1.4. THE LIMITS OF LOGIC.

Some people believe that logic can dissolve disagreements. Some also think that religious disagreements are at bottom intellectual. Both of these notions are wrong. The rules of deductive logic can do a lot in helping one think straight. When you say of someone, "That person is very logical," all you are saying is that the person's speaking or writing conforms to the rules of inference. The power of deductive logic is that if a person accepts the premises of an argument, then the rules of deductive logic compel him to accept the conclusion also. If he accepts the premises but rejects the conclusion of a valid argument, he can be accused of contradicting himself, and self-contradiction is the worst logical mistake one can commit. For example: Suppose your friend admits that A is taller than B and B is taller than C. Then he is compelled to admit that A is taller than C. Perhaps the most well-known example comes from Aristotelian deductive logic. Consider this syllogism:

(1) All men are mortal.
(2) Mr. X is a man.
(3) Therefore Mr. X is mortal.

Here, (1) and (2) are the premises of the syllogism. Whoever accepts (1) and (2) is compelled to accept (3). If a person says he accepts (1) and (2) but rejects (3), then we wonder about his thinking mechanism. Whether it is Aristotelian deductive logic or symbolic logic we are talking about, what we have said applies; the rules of deductive logic are very helpful in that they help us think straight.

But that is all that deductive logic can do, help you think straight. Deductive logic cannot compel you to accept any given belief system; its ability to help you make that kind of decision is at best minimal. What a person believes—whether in religion or in some other areas of life—is determined by other factors than deductive logic. Ultimately what belief system you embrace is not determined intellectually, if by intellectually we understand that which has to do with the mind, with logic. Attitudes, values, life styles, and other such things are often the primary determiners of the belief system a person embraces. When I was teaching in the university, I had occasion to present (outside the classroom) the Bible's plan of salvation to a third-year college student. This young man was a sharp one; he was a scholar of a certain company. In several conversations I presented the basics of salvation. In our last conversation I asked him if he would receive Christ as his Saviour and Lord. He said he would not. I asked him if he had understood what I had been saying and he said he had. And I had no doubt that he had understood all I had said to him; he was a sharp young man. Why would he not receive Christ as Saviour and Lord? His answer was something like this: "I can accept Christ as Saviour because of his death for sinners. But I cannot honestly accept Him as Lord if that means I have to surrender the governance of my life to him. I cannot give up my independence and let Jesus Christ direct my life. And if part of being a Christian is to let Jesus Christ direct my life, then I cannot accept Christ." He did not. Now here we have a man who rejected Christ. Was it because of faulty thinking on his part? No. He had a clear understanding of what I had told him. He correctly saw that to be a serious Christian it was necessary for him to let Jesus Christ direct his life. What made him reject Christ as Savior and Lord was the great value he placed on his personal independence. Logic can only help one understand a belief system and its implications; it cannot make him embrace it. In many situations in life logic cannot determine what you are to accept or reject.

1.5. THE IMPORTANCE OF CLARIFICATION.

Let us think on the following words of a contemporary analytic philosopher: [5]

> Now, analytic philosophy does not, indeed, have the same social function as some speculative philosophies of the past may have had. . . . . Analytic philosophy can hardly affect society in such direct ways. But its indirect function of curing people from intellectual confusions through special attention to the inexhaustible sources of abusing language, and of producing habits of sober, clear thinking and speaking—is it really of no social consequence?

Some people are impatient with the analytic philosopher's preoccupation with clarity. They say logical or linguistic analysis is barren, hence useless. But to say that is to miss the contribution of logical/linguistic analysis.

That contribution is the emphasis on clarity. Analytic/ linguistic philosophers believe that many of the persistent problems in the history of thought persist because of the lack of emphasis on clarity.

This is true not only in philosophy but also in other areas of thought, such as theology. In 1957 Dr. Edward J. Young, a theologian, speaking about the debate on inerrancy, wrote:[6]

> In present discussions of the Bible, both the words infallibility [sic] and inerrancy [sic] are often used without attempt at definition. The result is that much confusion has adhered and does adhere to current discussions of inspiration. There is not much point in talking of an infallible and inerrant Bible, unless we know what the words mean. (Emphasis mine)

Now that is a theologian talking. Sometimes a lot of discussion or debate succeeds only in making confusion worse because the parties to the discussion or debate have not taken the trouble to get clear of the words (especially the key words) and sentences used in the discussion. Some people think that bothering about words is a waste of time. "We are interested in ideas, not words," some might say. "Let's get on with the ideas." But the thing is that in communicating ideas we use words. There is nothing else we can use. We can use gestures to communicate, yes, but no one would prefer gestures to words. So whether we like it or not, we have to bother about the words and sentences we use in communicating ideas. We want the hearer or reader to understand accurately the idea we are trying to communicate; we want to make sure that all parties to the discussion or debate are clear as to what is being meant by each speaker. How easily confusion sets in.

A good number of years ago I sat down with a Christian who was a third- year college student who (I had been told) was "losing his faith" because of ideas he had encountered in his studies. I asked him to tell me what it was that bothered his faith. As I listened I saw that it was Bertrand Russell's views that bothered him. I asked him to tell me <u>exactly</u> what it was in Russell's philosophy that weakened his Christian beliefs and why. I listened some more. As he told me more, I came to the conclusion that the real problem was that he had not quite understood some of Russell's ideas and how those ideas related specifically to Christian beliefs.

Many times what is needed is <u>clarification</u> of the ideas involved, both the Christian ideas and the secular ideas. It is very important to see exactly how ideas relate to each other. In the flow of conversation people sometimes respond to a point without first taking the time to <u>clarify</u> the point under consideration. An assertion is made or a question is asked by the other person and one hurries to give an answer. Not taking time to make sure that the two discussants understand a given word or sentence <u>in the same way</u> often gives rise to confusion or misunderstanding. In the interest of accurate communication of ideas, it is necessary to clarify ideas before giving answers or making comments.

CHAPTER TWO
SCIENCE AND CHRISTIAN FAITH

The title of this chapter is not the usual way of referring to this subject. The usual pair is science/religion instead of science/Christian faith. Tad Clements, who wrote the article on this subject for the 1985 Encyclopedia of Unbelief, titles his article "Religion Vs. Science." Bertrand Russell's book on the subject is titled Religion and Science. I have chosen to speak of science and Christian faith instead of science and religion for the following reason. The word "religion" is today used by people to mean different things. Most of the time the word "religion" is used to apply to any one of Christianity, Islam, Buddhism and other so-called world religions. But there are other uses today of the word "religion." There are even people today who would say a person's religion is whatever occupies center stage in his life, in which case money or power or fame could be one's religion. And there are other uses of "religion." In his article, Clements acknowledges the ambiguity of the word "religion"; so he states that in his article he limits the term "religion" to "supernaturalistic religions, that is to religions in which belief in some reality allegedly above or beyond nature predominates." I find that the assertions and arguments Clements presents in his article apply properly to Christian belief. To avoid the ambiguity inherent in the word "religion," I prefer to speak of science and Christian faith. (The arguments used by unbelievers who discuss this subject generally apply to the Christian faith even if they prefer to speak of religion.)

What is the central issue here? To be sure there are a number of questions one can raise when thinking of the subject science/Christian belief. Here we want to focus our attention on the central issue. From my listening and reading it seems that what people consider to be the central issue is whether science conflicts with Christian belief. Dr. Tad Clements, Professor of Philosophy at the State University of New York at Brockton, thinks that is the central question. So does Dr. Isaac Asimov. So here we will focus on this question. (Some use the word "incompatible"; others use the word "conflict." Chapter 1 of Russell's book Religion and Science is titled "Grounds of Conflict.")

Before we go any further, let us distinguish science and nature, or science and what science investigates. This distinction is very important in our discussion of the question of whether science and Christian faith conflict, whether they are incompatible.

What is science? First, let us consult the dictionary. Webster's New Twentieth Century Dictionary defines "science" as follows: "1. originally, state or fact of knowing; knowledge, often as opposed to intuition, belief, etc.) 2. systematized knowledge derived from observation, and experimentation carried on in order to determine the nature or principles of what is being studied. 3. a branch of knowledge or study, especially one concerned with establishing, and systematizing facts, principles, and methods, and by experiments and hypotheses; as the science of music. 4. (a) the systematized knowledge of nature and the physical world; (b) any branch of this. 5. skill, technique, or ability based upon training, discipline, and experience; often somewhat humorous, as, the science of boxing." In his book The Natural Sciences and the Christian Message, the believer Dr. Albert van der Ziel, Professor of Electrical Engineering at the University of Minnesota, defines science thus: "We thus define science as a systematic investigation, interrelation and exposition of a certain field of human experience." Ven der Ziel does not like the expression "the scientific method"; he thinks that "each field [of investigation] brings with it its own method of investigation." [1] In his book Science and Man the unbeliever Tad Clements speaks of science as "a body of knowledge" (p. 5). In his book Religion and Science, the unbeliever Bertrand Russell, one of the great philosophers of the 20th century, defines " science" this way: "Science is the attempt to discover, by means of observation, and reasoning based upon it, first, particular facts about the world, and then laws connecting facts with one another and (in fortunate cases) making it possible to predict occurrences."[2] Now one thing that is clear in the definition of the word "science" is that science is not the same as nature; science is the investigation of nature or the outcome of such investigation; science is not what is investigated. The expression "natural science" accents the fact that scientists study nature. The work of the scientist and the knowledge resulting from scientific activity must then be distinguished from nature, or from that which scientists study.

Another distinction must be made before we attempt to answer the central question. We should distinguish Christian faith from its objects, namely, God, Jesus Christ, Holy Spirit, revelation. Christian faith is not the same thing as God; it is not the same thing as Jesus Christ; neither is it the same thing as the Holy Spirit; neither is it revelation. Christian faith is not the same thing as the Bible. Christian faith is the believer's belief and practice. That which the believer believes is one thing; his believing and the way of life that results from his believing is a different thing.

Why are we pushing these distinctions? The reason is that making these distinctions is an important preliminary to our answering the central issue of whether science conflicts with Christian faith. Now our answer can be given. There is no conflict between God, Jesus Christ, the Holy Spirit and revelation on the one hand and nature (or cosmos) on the other. If God, Jesus Christ, the Holy Spirit and revelation are real, then they are there in the same manner that the universe is there. And there is no conflict between them. If, as the Christian believes, God exists and has made Himself known through the prophets and primarily in and through Jesus

Christ, there is no conflict between God and Christ on the one hand and the cosmos on the other.

The story is quite different when it is science and Christian faith that we are talking about. If one applies the methods and criteria of science to all areas of thought and action, then science conflicts with Christian faith. The conflict is fundamental and very serious. Even the definitions of some words are affected by the conflict; for example, the words "knowledge," "rational," "reasonable," "good grounds" and possibly others are affected seriously by the conflict. The incompatibility is fundamental because it has to do with methodology and criteria. The conflict will become clear as we proceed in this chapter.

Let us start with the subject of scientific methodology. The atheist Dr. Isaac Asimov, Professor of Biochemistry at Boston University School of Medicine, writes: ". . . science deals with those aspects of the universe that can be observed by the senses, that can be measured by instruments in a reproducible manner with results that do not deviate erratically from time to time or place to place or experimenter to experimenter."[3] Note the key phrases in this passage from Asimov: "can be observed by the senses," "can be measured by instruments in a reproducible manner." In other words, science does not deal with entities that cannot be observed by the senses or measured by instruments in a reproducible manner. If there are any entities that cannot be observed by the senses or measured by instruments in a reproducible manner, such entities are not dealt with by science—better, such entities cannot be dealt with by science.

Now what does this imply with respect to God? Clearly it implies that science cannot deal with God, since God is Spirit and therefore cannot be observed by the senses or measured by the scientist's instruments. Therefore science cannot say anything about God; science cannot but find God-talk meaningless. On the question of whether God exists or not science is completely dumb.

As far as Asimov is concerned, there is a conflict between science and Christian faith in that the Christian makes assertions about God; indeed, the Christian's life centers on God; the more serious a Christian is in his faith, the more his daily decisions are motivated by considerations that center on God. But to one who <u>limits</u> himself to scientific methodology (as described by Asimov), such a way of life is utterly foolish. Isn't it foolish to pivot your daily life on belief in something that you cannot know anything about? The logician would say, How can you believe something you can know nothing about? Belief presupposes that that which is believed is at least understood.

In <u>The Necessity of Atheism</u>, David Brooks, an unbeliever medical doctor, writes: "truth to the scientific mind is something provisional, a hypothesis that for the present moment best conforms to the recognized tests. It is an evolving conception in a constantly changing universe."[4] Here we see a clear conflict between science and Christian faith. Whereas, according to Brooks, tentativeness, provisionality, is inherent in science's conception of truth, in Christian faith the believer is fully committed to the permanence of the truths he finds in the Bible. It does not make sense to speak of <u>revising</u> the revelation that is recorded in the Bible. So committed is the Christian that he bets his life on the Bible truths. The notion of provisionality, of tentativeness, is meaningless when applied to Christian faith.

In its ideal sense, Christian faith resembles marriage in its ideal aspect. When a man and a woman pledge before God and the assembled witnesses that they will stick together "in sickness and in health, till death do us part," they are putting their earthly destinies on the line. Again, we are talking about marriage in its ideal sense, in which the parties mean what they say when they recite their pledge to each other. There is a finality in the attitudes of the parties.

Now let us listen to the unbeliever Dr. Tad Clements. In his book <u>Science and Man</u>, Clements writes[5]

. . . the <u>assumptions</u> that all events have causes (of some sort), i. e., the doctrine of determinism, is warranted. It is warranted as a methodological <u>postulate</u>. If there were

and event, @, which had no antecedent determinants, it
would not be possible to understand it by means of
scientific methods. If it were impossible, even in
principle, to understand @ by scientific methods, @
would be essentially [Clements' emphasis] enigmatic. If
it were essentially [Clement' emphasis] enigmatic, it
could never be incorporated within any system of natural
knowledge. But the purpose of all natural sciences is,
among other things, to explain systematically. Hence,
science as an enterprise is committed to the doctrine that
all events have cause, because science is committed to
systematic explanation. (Unless indicated otherwise,
emphases are mine.)

In the first sentence of this passage, we are told that
determinism is an assumption. As we stated in Chapter 1, an
assumption is a methodology, a criterion, a principle, a fact or
something else that is taken by the writer or speaker as true and
used as such without the benefit of argument or evidence. The
truth of what is assumed is taken for granted. It helps to make
things clear by stating, as Clements does, that determinism is
an assumption of science.

In the first sentence of this passage, Clements says that the
doctrine that all events have causes—the doctrine of determinism—is warranted. What kinds of things will science admit as
possible causes? The causes must in every case be natural.
What is "natural"? From the tenor of chapter 2 of Clements'
Science and Man we can conclude that Clements would define
"natural" as meaning that which can be observed by means of
the senses (including instrument readings). In other words,
Clements is saying that there cannot be any events whose
causes are not observable by means of the senses. That means
that the only reality science can know is such as can be
observed. Another way of saying that is that the only reality
that can be known is that which can be known by means of the
techniques of science.

"Hasn't Clements thereby limited reality?" He has certainly limited the reality that can be known; he has not limited

reality—he cannot! As described by Clements, science cannot say whether there is any reality outside of that which can be known by means of the techniques of science. For example, science cannot say whether God exists. Since God is Spirit and therefore in principle unobservable by the senses, then science has nothing to say about God; science can neither affirm nor deny that God exists.

"But isn't the scientist's world limited? Isn't his view of reality quite limited?" It is. The methodological and criterial assumptions of science (as described by Clements) make science agnostic about that portion of reality which is not amenable to the techniques of science. It is a limited world indeed.

Take the case of miracles. The concept miracle has two essential elements. First, a miracle is an event, a happening that occurs in the world. The other element is that it is caused by God. Now as far as the first element is concerned, the scientist and the Christian can make the same sense of it; in so far as a miracle is an event, it is observable by means of the senses. Moses saw the burning bush. On the road to Damascus, when Christ spoke to Saul of Tarsus, Saul heard the voice and saw the light. People saw the empty tomb where Jesus' dead body had been laid. Many people saw the risen Christ at different times in different places. As events miracles are no less observable than non-miraculous events. The scientist should have no trouble making sense of miracles as events. A burning bush is a burning bush to the believer as well as to the unbeliever. Of course the unbeliever scientist will not call miraculous events miracles, since the concept miracle essentially involves the supernatural.

When it comes to the second element in the concept miracle (that God is the cause of miracles), the scientist and the Christian part ways: the scientist cannot make sense of the Christian's statement that God caused the miraculous event. The scientist cannot deny that God caused the event in question; one can deny only what is meaningful to one.

The scientist's world is limited by his adoption of empiricist methods and criteria. If there are real entities which are not knowable by means of the techniques of science, those entities are beyond the reach of science. Now some people might say that aside from God, there are other real entities which are beyond the reach of science. Satan is one such reality.

Scientists will say that the element of repeatability lies at the heart of scientific activity. Testability presupposes the possibility of other scientists repeating the experiment in question or the same scientist repeating the experiment he has performed. If an experiment cannot be repeated by other scientists, its results are seriously suspect. So when Clements speaks of the assumption of science that all events have natural causes, we must keep in mind that "natural" involves at least the element of being observable by the senses and also the element of repeatability.

When we introduce the element of repeatability, we have introduced another reason why science cannot make sense of miracle talk. Miracles are unique events. There is no possibility of "redoing" a miraculous event. Jesus was raised by God from the dead and that happened once and once only. The water in the jars at the wedding feast in Cana that became wine was the only water that became wine; even at that particular hour water in all other places in the world tasted water and not wine. Now if science cannot make sense of something which cannot be "rerun" then here is another reason why science cannot make sense of miracle talk.

From the fact that science cannot make sense of miracle talk it does not follow that miracle talk is meaningless, period. It is important to say this. We must remind the scientist that his language-game is only one of many actual language-games in the world. If in the scientist's language-game miracle talk is nonsense, that's because science has adopted empiricist methods and criteria. But other language-games do not have to adopt empiricist methods and criteria. Now let us be careful that no one language-game dictate to other language-games. No one language-game can claim that it is superior to other language-games. To make that claim requires a set of criteria accepted by all language-games, to which appeal can be made as to which language-game is the best or the superior one. In so far as each language-game exists for certain purposes, meets certain needs; and in so far as each language-game adopts methods and criteria suited to its peculiar goals or interests, the different actual language-games in the world are logically on the same footing with each other.

The analogy provided by the games played by athletes helps us here. Each of basketball, baseball, football, tennis, and other games played by athletes has its own rules and criteria. It does not make sense to speak of any one game being superior to any other game. How do we determine that? What criteria do we judge by? The criteria are internal to the different games; there are no specific criteria which apply to all games. That is why if a poll is taken, there will be those who will say their No. 1 game is basketball while there will be those whose favorite game is something else. There are no criteria that can "compel" everyone to vote any one game as the superior one. Now I want to say that there is a very strong analogy here with the fact that science and Christianity are language-games. Logically, as language-games, they are on the same footing; each has its own methods and criteria. And the criteria that apply to science must not be imposed on the activities that go on within the language-game of Christianity—and vice versa.

The last point we want to notice in the passage we have quoted from Clements is Clements' idea of the scientist being "committed to the doctrine that all events have causes." Now commitment pertains to the scientist's attitude. It does not pertain to methods or criteria. Commitment has to do with the scientist as a person. Here we see that science (as portrayed by Clements) has admitted into its dictionary a non-natural element. Commitment to scientific methodology or scientific explanation is not a natural element since one can be a human being without being so committed; being committed to scientific methods or criteria is not an essential part of human nature.

It is interesting that Clements speaks of the scientist's

being <u>committed</u> to scientific methodology. In this aspect we find a similarity between science and Christian faith: both the scientist and the Christian are committed persons. But they differ fundamentally as to what they are committed to. The Christian is committed to doing God's will day by day; the Christian is committed to allowing Jesus Christ to be Lord of his life; the Christian is committed to making the Bible his rule of faith and action. The scientist is committed to methods and criteria that rule out even the meaningfulness of God-talk. Here we see how fundamental and serious is the conflict between science and Christian faith.

Now we raise what to us is an important question related to Clements' talk of the scientist's commitment to empirical methods and criteria. The question is this. Is it possible for the same person to be a sincere Christian and at the same time a serious respectable scientist? To this question Clements would answer no. Our answer is yes. We believe that a person can seriously engage in the scientific enterprise without being committed to applying scientific methods and criteria to all areas of thought and action—without <u>limiting</u> himself to the methods and criteria of science. Now some will object to this and argue that it is possible for the same person to be both a Christian and a scientist only if he allows <u>himself</u> to be compartmentalized, in which case he cannot be a really serious and respectable scientist. In reply to this objection, we want to ask what the compartmentalization spoken about actually is. The person cannot be compartmentalized—whatever that means. His mind cannot be "divided up into compartments"—whatever that means. It is not that one <u>part</u> of him is a scientist and the other <u>part</u> a Christian—that does not make sense. Does compartmentalization mean that he is a scientist during the hours and minutes that he is "doing science" and a Christian at all other times? But in that case, there are times when he is not a Christian. He is not a Christian from 8 AM through 5 PM Monday through Friday; he is a Christian from 5 PM through 8 AM the following day Monday through Friday and from 5 PM Friday through 8 AM the following Monday. He is also a Christian during holidays and vacation days. That sounds like a joke. I find it difficult to understand what the unbeliever means by compartmentalization here. <u>What</u> is compartmentalized? And what is that activity or process which is here called compartmentalization? Until the term "compartmentalization" is clarified, we are at a loss to respond specifically.

But the charge of compartmentalization is made by some unbelievers. So let us try to make a reply.

Instead of talking about compartmentalization, it is more helpful to speak of the same individual giving a scientific explanation at time T-1 and a Christian (or Biblical) explanation at time T-2. In this way we are not "dividing up" the individual; he remains one and the same individual at T-1 and T-2. His whole being, shall we say, is intact at both T-1 and T-2. But at different times and in different situations the same individual can be giving now a scientific explanation and now a Biblical one. It is thus that it is possible for the same individual to be both a serious and respectable scientist and a serious Christian. No compartmentalization is necessary.

It goes without saying that confusion can arise when it is not made clear what kind of explanation he is giving. The categories he uses when giving a scientific explanation will of course be quite different from the categories he uses when giving a Biblical explanation. As long as the individual does not mix categories, there is no difficulty in the idea of the same individual being a serious scientist and at the same time a sincere Christian. The scientist who is a Christian can offer Christian and scientific explanations at different times and in different situations.

Stating our position can be helped by the use of an example. Let us take as our example the wedding feast at Cana in Galilee, narrated in the Gospel of John chapter 2. The narrative tells us that there was a wedding feast at Cana in Galilee to which Jesus and his disciples were invited. At a certain point during the feast, the wine ran out. Now there were six stone jars, each capable of holding from twenty to thirty gallons. When it was known that the wine had run out, Jesus told the servants to fill the jars with water. The servants filled up the jars, after which Jesus told them to draw some out and to take it to the steward of the feast. A servant took water from one of the jars to the steward of the feast. When the steward tasted the water given to him, it was wine; in fact it was better wine than the one that had run out. The steward expressed to the bridegroom his surprise at the fact that the better wine was served last—contrary to the usual practice. That's the story.

For convenience in deploying our example, let us designate the time before the water was tasted by the steward as T-1 (time-1) and the time after the steward tasted the water (=wine) as T-2 (time-2). Now let us imagine that in that feast there were two Ph. D.s in chemistry, one a Christian and the other an unbeliever. And let us imagine that they did chemical analysis of the properties of the water at T-1. At T-1 their analyses showed that the liquid in the jars had the properties of water. Then let us imagine that the two scientists did chemical analysis of the liquid in the glass that the steward tasted and they both found that the liquid had the properties of wine. Up to that point, both chemists were doing pure scientific analysis. They used the same instruments. And they had exactly the same findings as to the properties of the liquids analyzed. So far the two scientists had no disagreement at all. Now we ask both scientists: "Sirs, how do you account for the difference in properties?" (You see, the liquid that the servants placed in the six jars on Jesus' instruction was water; the servants knew it was water. But what the steward tasted was wine, not water. And yet the liquid he tasted came from one of the jars into which the servants had poured water just moments earlier.) What would the two scientists say? (Let us call the Christian chemist Dr. C and the unbeliever chemist Dr. U.) Dr. U would probably say, "It puzzles me; in fact, I can't make any sense of it." But Dr. C, who believes in the possibility of God causing events in the world, answers, "Well, speaking as a Christian, my answer is that God had performed a miracle in our midst; God changed what was water into wine. I have no problem understanding that." That's the difference between the unbeliever scientist and the

Christian scientist. Now we must emphasize that Dr. C's explanation is of course not a scientific explanation— it cannot be. Science cannot make sense of what happened. As an unbeliever scientist, and having been quite surprised by what happened, Dr. U might suggest that he and Dr. C conduct experiments. And Dr. C would tell Dr. U that no such "experiment" is possible; miracles are unique events. There is no such thing as "redoing" a miracle, or "repeating the experiment." Given that answer, Dr. U would say that in that case, the question why the water became wine is not a scientific question. Dr. U would say one reason that question is not a question in science is that neither he nor Dr. C could repeat the experiment at other times or in other places. Another reason Dr. U would say our question is not a scientific one is that the causal explanation we asked for is not admissible into the scientist's vocabulary of systematic explanation.

Now we ask: Was Dr. C less of a scientist in this situation than Dr. U? Was Dr. C's chemical analysis less respectable than that of Dr. U? Not at all. They did the same things in their analysis; they used the same instruments. And they came to the same conclusions as to the properties of the liquids analyzed. As far as the scientific activity was concerned, Dr. C and Dr. U did equally respectable jobs as scientists. Dr. U could not have accused Dr. C of doing a less reliable scientific investigation, a less respectable scientific job. But when it came to giving an account of why the water changed properties, Dr. U was not even able to make sense of the phenomenon. They did not disagree really, since Dr. U did not give an explanation. Of course, if Dr. C limited himself strictly to scientific methodology and criteria; if Dr. C applied the methods and criteria of science to the situation, he could not have offered the explanation he gave, since the methods and criteria of science cannot tolerate any unverifiable entities such as God nor the causal efficacy of any unverifiable entities. Scientific methodology requires that the data or entities admitted must be capable of being observed by the senses and measured by means of the instruments of science.

So God-related explanations are out as far as scientific methodology and criteria go. That is why in giving his account of what happened, Dr. C had to say "speaking as a Christian." It was necessary to say that, to make sure that the people understood that the explanation he was giving was a Christian explanation and not a scientific one.

In what respect did our two scientists differ? They differed in that Dr. C was willing to bring God into his explanation of the change of properties of the water; Dr. U was not willing to introduce God into the situation, since Dr. U was an unbeliever. As a rigorous unbeliever scientist Dr. U would not admit any unverifiable entities such as God. The only course open to him was to admit his inability to even make sense of the phenomenon. But, we must repeat, Dr. U could not have accused Dr. C of having done a less serious, less respectable, job as far as Dr. C's chemical analysis of the liquids was concerned.

The unbeliever might object. "But can a scientist speak as a Christian?" Of course the scientist cannot speak as a Christian when giving a scientific explanation; neither can he speak as a scientist when giving a Christian explanation. The reason is that there is a logical incompatibility between the categories of Christian faith and those of scientific methodology. But the scientist who is a Christian can speak as a Christian when giving a Christian explanation; there is nothing internally incoherent about that. But always it must be clearly understood that one is giving a Christian explanation and not a scientific one. Within the context of the methods and criteria of science, Christian explanations are meaningless. The language-game of science cannot tolerate the categories of the Bible.

Then this question arises: Must the scientist at all times and in all situations limit himself to scientific explanations? Must the scientist at all times and in all situations impose on whatever is at hand the criteria of science? For us this is a very important question. Our answer is: There is nothing in scientific methodology that logically necessitates that in all situations and at all times the scientist apply the methods and criteria of science. To say that is to assume that all subject matter and all entities are amenable to, capable of being dealt with by means of, scientific methodology. That assumption is highly questionable. For one thing that assumption presumes that God does not exist. Science logically is incapable of denying that God exists. It is one thing to deny the possibility of knowing that X exists and another thing to deny that X exists. Science denies the possibility of knowing anything about the supernatural but science cannot deny that the supernatural exists or does certain things in the world.

There is no inherent contradiction in the idea of the same person being a serious and respectable scientist and at the same time a Christian. I personally know several persons who are Ph.D.s in various areas in science and who are serious Christians. But the unbeliever might object by saying, "But if a person is a serious Christian, then he cannot be a serious scientist." The unbeliever can raise that objection if and only if he defines "serious scientist" to mean a person who will not admit any explanation that admits any unverifiable entities such as God. In that case, the quarrel is about the definition of the term "serious scientist." As we have said earlier, the conflict between science and Christian faith is so fundamental that it even affects the definitions of certain key terms.

The unbeliever might object to our idea that the scientist speaking as a Christian can give a Christian explanation. He might say that that is compartmentalization. But in our example, Dr. C was one whole person when he was doing his analysis of the liquids as well as when he was giving a Christian explanation. He was at both times speaking as one person—not as a divided person, whatever that means. We find the idea of compartmentalization difficult to understand. But we have no difficulty with the idea that the same person who is a scientist can in certain situations give a Christian explanation. The same person can be a serious, respectable scientist and at the same time a sincere and serious follower of Christ.

CHAPTER THREE

MIRACLES

When it comes to miracles, what is the issue that divides Christians and unbelievers? It is important to ask this question right at the start, lest we forget what it is that the two sides disagree about at bottom. The one issue, it seems to me, is this: Are miracles possible? On this question Christians and unbelievers are clearly divided, with Christians saying yes and unbelievers saying no.

The real issue is not how many miracles are admitted or whether it is only the Biblical miracles or also those reported in post-Biblical times. These are subsidiary issues and we will not deal with them here. The issue we want to confront here is the issue of the possibility of miracles. (Of course we are here talking of practical, not logical, possibility, since we are concerned with matters of fact.)

The Christian does not have to defend all miracle reports. In fact, to defend the affirmative side on this issue the Christian needs to defend the occurrence of just one miracle. One occurrence is enough to prove possibility. If miracles are impossible, then there cannot be one occurrence. If there has been at least one occurrence of a miracle, then we know that miracles are possible. So in our discussion we will focus on just one example, namely, the resurrection of Jesus. We have chosen as our own example the resurrection of Jesus because it is the central miracle in Christianity. The preaching of the apostles centered on the fact that Christ had been raised from the dead.

The philosopher David Hume (died 1776) is generally considered to have been the unbeliever to deliver the first real hard blow on the Christian belief in miracles. In the history of philosophy Hume is considered one of the greats. He was famous for his theory of knowledge. In the 20th century some empiricist philosophers look up to Hume as their father. Antony Flew, who is still living at this writing, is one of the contemporary philosophers strongly influenced by Hume's epistemology.

As can be expected, it was Hume's epistemology that led to his denial of the possibility of miracles. So first let us do a brief review of his theory of knowledge before we do our critique. In brief, Hume's theory of knowledge is as follows. All knowledge of matters of fact comes from experience. As we use our various sense organs, Hume said, we get "impressions" (his technical word). For example, you look at a ball that is sitting on the table in front of you. You get the impressions of shape, size, color, hardness (if you touch the ball), smell (if you smell it), weight (if you lift it). Hours after you saw the ball, you might think of it and you have (in the mind) a group of "ideas" (again, Hume's technical term); each of the ideas corresponds to an impression you had when you were looking at, touching, smelling, and lifting the ball. Ideas are weakened impressions that are left in the mind. Now do that for all the things you get to know. No matter how complex the matters of fact, sense experience is the only way you get to know anything about them.

Do all the complex ideas we have correspond to actual things we have perceived? No, not necessarily. Hume's example of the golden mountain is famous. He said we can have an idea (a complex idea) of a golden mountain although there are no actual golden mountains in the world. We get our idea of a golden mountain as follows: We have seen gold or at least gold-colored things. And we have seen mountains. Those experiences have left ideas in us. Now we can combine the idea of the color of gold and the ideas of the size and shape of a mountain. The combination of ideas (which is a complex idea) is what Hume calls the idea of a golden mountain. In this way we can have ideas of things that do not actually exist, things we do not actually experience. But those complex ideas are derived from our actual experiences. There are no ideas which are not traced to impressions and there are no impressions which are not due to the use of our senses.

The other part of Hume's radical empiricism is his theory about cause and effect, or about laws of nature. What do we mean by cause and by effect? How do we know that A is the cause of B? The answer, as we would expect, makes use of the theory about impressions and ideas. According to Hume, as we employ our various senses we notice that some kinds of impressions are constantly and regularly conjoined—those are his technical words. There are, for example, certain colors that in our observation always go with certain shapes and sizes. As we observe more and more, we come upon more instances of these constant and regular conjunctions of types of impressions. If we have noticed A-impressions precede B-impressions constantly and regularly, then we in time come to think that A is the cause of B. The more times we have observed the conjunction between A-impressions and B-impressions and provided we have not observed any exceptions, the more firm our belief that A is the cause of B. Or we come to believe that there is a causal connection between A and B. In time we come to speak of a necessary <u>causal connection</u> between A-impressions and B-impressions, or, simply, between A and B.

One observation of A-impressions preceding or being accompanied by B-impressions is not enough for us to say that there is a causal connection between A and B; there must be many experiences of the conjunction. This point is very important in Hume's theory. The more times we have observed A-impressions being conjoined with B-impressions, and the more uniform the conjunction, the greater our belief that A and B are causally connected.

Do we <u>observe</u> the causal <u>connection</u> of A and B? No, we do not. What we observe are only "loose" and "separate" impressions; "loose" and "separate" are Hume's technical words. We never observe two impressions somehow tied to each other—never. What we observe are only conjunctions of impressions in time and space. As far as our observation goes, impressions are always loose and separate. What we do observe is that some kinds of impressions are constantly and regularly conjoined in terms of time and space.

If we never observe impressions <u>connected</u> to each other, where do we get the idea of the <u>necessity of connection</u> between cause and effect? Where does the necessity come from? Hume's answer is that necessity of causal connection is contributed by the mind; it is not in nature. After we have observed A-impressions constantly and regularly conjoined in time and space with B-impressions, the next time we see an A-impression we <u>expect</u> to see a B-impression. Our minds establish an <u>association</u> between A and B. And in time this connection is thought to be necessary; in time we come to think that A and B are necessarily causally connected. But in actuality A and B are not connected; actually the only observable thing about A and B is that A-impressions and B-impressions have been observed to be constantly and regularly conjoined.

A <u>law of nature</u>, Hume holds, is a causal connection between types of impressions. For example (this is our own example) we have seen many a man die and buried. We (that is, you and I) have never seen a single man die and become alive again. Our experience has been uniform. Given that <u>uniform</u> experience, Hume would say it is a <u>law of nature</u> that a dead man remains dead. We must emphasize that for Hume "law of nature" is <u>defined</u> in terms of the constant and regular conjunction of impressions. Also, we want to emphasize that the idea of uniformity of experience lies behind the Humean notion of law of nature; in fact "law of nature" = "uniform experience."

That, in brief, is Hume's radical empiricism. All knowledge derives from sense experience. Every claim to knowledge about matters of fact is rejected if it cannot be shown to be <u>based ultimately on observation</u>.

Now given that epistemological theory, how does Hume explain phenomena? He explains events always in terms of the laws of nature—<u>always</u> in terms of the constant and regular conjunctions of types of impressions: always in terms of observation.

Let us now ask how this theory deals with the question of the possibility of miracles. Hume discusses the subject of miracles in Section X of his <u>An Enquiry Concerning Human Understanding</u>. (Our page numbers are based on the Open Court paperback edition, 1966.)

On p. 126 Hume writes: "A miracle is a violation of the laws of nature." Then in a footnote on p. 127 he gives us his definition of "miracle": "A miracle may be accurately defined, a transgression of a law of nature by a particular volition of the Deity, or by the interposition of some invisible agent." The question we want to ask concerning this definition is what Hume means by "violation" and by "transgression." I think he means one thing by these two words. What he means must be gleaned from his conception of "law of nature." For Hume a law of nature is a pattern of observed regular and constant conjunction of types of impressions. On p. 126 he uses the expression "a firm and unalterable experience"; on p. 127 he speaks of "a uniform experience." For example, it is a law of nature that dead men remain dead because it "has never been observed in any age or country" "that a dead man should come to life." Since Hume <u>defines</u> "miracle" as a transgression of the laws of nature, then a dead man's coming to life again is a miracle, since it is contrary to the uniform experience of mankind that a dead man remains dead.

Before we go any further, let us pause to comment on Hume's view. Our first comment is on Hume's use of the words "violation" and "transgression" in his definition of "miracle." Here the word "violation" or "transgression" is problematic <u>within</u> the context of Hume's explicitly stated theory of knowledge. In its ordinary use "violation" contemplates a prescriptive law. The normal use of "violation" is in such sentences as "Driving two hundred kilometers per hour is a violation of law." The law which one violates is one normally passed by a legislature; perhaps in some cases the law is laid down as a decree by some proper authority.

In Hume's own theory there is no room for the notion of legislation or prescription in nature. He says all we observe are <u>loose and separate</u> impressions. We observe nothing else. And observation is the only means whereby we come to know any matter of fact. True, we observe constant and regular conjunctions of types of impressions, but still impressions come <u>one by one</u>, loose and separate. Impressions are not connected. The conjunction is only temporal and spatial. In such a context the idea of prescription or legislation is simply out of place. So we are quite surprised that Hume would call a miracle a "violation" or a "transgression" of the laws of nature. In Hume's own theory, we never observe anything that we can call nature. Hume's talk of nature surprises us. What is that? How do we come to know that? Nowhere in his theory is there any talk of any other thing than loose and separate impressions. Now if there is no nature, how can there be laws of nature?

Why does Hume, who otherwise is a careful writer, make a poor choice of a word? Why does he talk about laws of nature when his own theory does not refer to nature at all? I have a suspicion as to why. I can think of two possible reasons why Hume would speak of laws <u>of nature</u>. One possible reason is that Hume had really not abandoned in his mind belief in the external world, in the world out there independent of the mind. Perhaps unconsciously Hume still believed in a world different from loose and separate impressions, a world <u>in which</u> loose and separate impressions occur. The first pages of his <u>Treatise</u> and the <u>Enquiry</u> show a credulous confidence in a Baconian nature.

My second guess is speculative. Perhaps Hume speaks of laws <u>of nature</u> because such a notion would give the observed conjunctions of loose and separate impressions a more stable status, as if laws of nature were there <u>in reality</u> existing (or subsisting) by themselves, independently of human thought. Such a situation would make the occurrence of miracles more unbelievable, since miracles, by Hume's definition, are violations of laws of nature. The more stable laws of nature are, the more unbelievable miracles are. The only trouble with that is that in Hume's theory there is no nature to speak of. If we take Hume's theory seriously, then we cannot speak of the laws of nature.

Let us comment now on Hume's factual assertion that it has never been observed anywhere at any time that a dead man came to life again. This, we must point out, is offered as a straightforward factual assertion. It is not argued. Neither does Hume present this claim as the conclusion of a factual investigation. It is given simply as a flat categorical assertion. We raise a strong objection here. The point of contention between Hume and us with respect to our prime example of a miracle (Jesus' resurrection) is precisely whether in fact Jesus died and became alive again. It is the Christian's belief that Jesus did die on the Cross, that he was buried, that he was in the grave three days, that on the third day his tomb was found empty, and that after the third day Jesus was seen a number of times by different people, at one time by a crowd of some five hundred persons. The Christian belief is based, of course, on the historical narratives that we read in the New Testament. We must emphasize that the narratives in the New Testament are historical. The narratives have it that there were people who were witnesses to the events surrounding the death and post-resurrection appearances of Jesus. Now in asserting that it has never been observed in any age in any country that a dead man came to life again Hume clearly implies that no one saw Jesus die and no one saw Jesus in his post-resurrection appearances. By his straightforward factual assertion Hume implies that all the New Testament narratives about the death, burial and post-resurrection appearances of Jesus are entirely false. Now that is a very big assertion. It is interesting to note that Hume makes that implied charge without bothering to do any kind of factual investigation. He simply states a factual assertion—as if the mere convenience of stating an assertion made the testimonies of many witnesses null and void! As if a simple straightforward assertion was sufficient to falsify all the New Testament narratives of the death, burial and post-resurrection appearances of the risen Christ. It is intriguing to me that in his chapter on miracles Hume does not make any reference to the resurrection of Jesus. If he wished to discredit the Christian belief in miracle, he should have at least made some reference to the resurrection of Jesus since that is the central miracle of the Christian religion. The focus of the preaching of the apostles was the resurrection of Jesus. How could Hume have thought that the resurrection of Jesus was not important at all? How could he have thought that it was so insignificant as not to merit a factual investigation?

As an empiricist, Hume's distinctive posture is observation. Now the New Testament narratives state that many people observed the death and then the post-resurrection appearances of Jesus. And Hume simply states in a flat straightforward assertion that it has NEVER been observed in any age in any country that a dead man came to life again. To have completely ignored the whole New Testament story of the death and the resurrection of Jesus is to have evaded a whole chunk of history, a chunk that has greatly influenced the course of world history.

If, as Hume clearly implies, the New Testament narratives of the death and resurrection of Jesus are entirely false, he should tell us at some length why he thinks the narratives are totally false. But Hume does not make any reference at all to the resurrection of Jesus—not a word in his entire chapter on miracles. Very strange, isn't it?

Over and over, the disciples of Jesus told the people they were witnesses to the death and the post-ressurection appearances of Jesus. And they did so under severe risk. They knew they were laying their lives on the line in insisting on preaching that Jesus was raised from the grave. The religious authorities warned them not to continue preaching that message; they were arrested, beaten, put in jail; some were stoned to death. But they continued telling people of their risen Lord. How could Hume have simply dismissed all that by a simple assertion—without the benefit of factual investigation? Very strange indeed.

What does Hume say about unique events? Nothing. All that we observe, says Hume, are loose and separate impressions. Types of impressions are observed to be in constant and regular conjunction.

But does Hume's theory preclude the occurrence of unique events such as the resurrection of Jesus? No, it does not—it cannot. There is nothing in Hume's theory that makes the occurrence of unique (unrepeated) events impossible. True, Hume defines miracle as a violation of the laws of nature. But all that that means is that miracles are contrary to the laws of nature, and what that means is that miracles do not conform to the observed patterns of constant and regular conjunctions of impressions. Granted that types of impressions occur in constant and regular conjunction. But the fact remains that according to Hume what we observe are loose and separate impressions. Now loose and separate impressions cannot preclude the occurrence of a unique event such as the resurrection of Jesus. True, a unique event does not conform to the pattern of constant and regular conjunctions of impressions, and that's because unique events are unique, they are not members of classes of impressions. The point we insist on is that the logic of loose and separate sense data is compatible with the occurrence of unique events such as the resurrection of Christ. There is nothing in Hume's theory that excludes the possibility of a unique event happening. Even if all that Hume's wise man has observed is the constant and regular conjunction of impressions, still the occurrence of a unique event remains not only logically but also practically possible. After all, observation is not legislation!

Hume's theory of knowledge is inadequate in that it leaves out unique phenomena. If a unique event occurs, Hume would not know what to say about it. All that he knows is that types of impressions are in constant and regular conjunction; the element of repetition is deeply embedded in Hume's epistemology. Since miracles are unique (nonrepeating) phenomena, Hume does not know how to deal with them. But at the same time, Hume's theory cannot rule out the occurrence of a unique event.

The concept miracle introduces into the language the idea that motive, or volition, is a legitimate explanation of events. It was God's will to raise Jesus from the dead. Now this kind of explanation Hume will reject, of course, since according to Hume's theory explanation always is in terms of laws of nature. Hume's theory of explanation always fits the phenomenon within the framework of a law of nature. Talk about God is pure nonsense in Hume's epistemology. But reference to purpose is one of the recognized types of explanation. A. Wolf, a professor of logic and scientific method, writes: "In the study of certain biological phenomena, and above all, in the study of human experiences and activities, individual and social, it is scarcely possible to dispense with the conception of purpose, if we are to have really adequate explanations. Even the most violent opponent of teleological explanation, even the most thoroughgoing determinist, would hardly be flattered if his writing and other activities were described as guided by no aim, and devoid of all purpose!" [1] If human activities are explained in terms of purpose, God's doings also can be so explained. God is described in the Bible as having will, purpose. Now the accurate way to refer to the resurrection of Jesus is that Jesus was raised (by God) from the dead. At Romans 6:4 we read that God raised Jesus from the dead in order that "we too might walk in newness of life." Jesus' resurrection was willed by God. In the definition of "miracle" God figures as an essential element; a miracle takes place by the will of God.

On p. 127 Hume writes: "The plain consequence is (and it is a general maxim worthy of our attention), 'That no testimony is sufficient to establish a miracle unless the testimony be of such a kind, that its falsehood would be more miraculous, than the fact, which it endeavors to establish; and even in that case there is a mutual destruction of arguments, and the superior only gives us an assurance suitable to that degree of force, which remains, after deducting the inferior.'" The first part of this sentence is quite problematic; let us examine it closely. As we have seen, according to Hume a miracle is a violation of a law of nature, and a law of nature is a uniform experience of mankind. Hume says that the testimony that seeks to establish a miracle succeeds in establishing it only if _its_ falsehood is more miraculous than the event it is endeavoring to establish as miraculous. But X can be more miraculous than Y only if in the first place X is itself miraculous, since only that which is miraculous can be more miraculous. Since Hume defines a miracle as a violation of a law of nature, then for the falsehood of the testimony to be miraculous, it is necessary that there be a law of nature that the testimony's falsehood violates. So we ask: Can there be a law of nature that the testimony's falsehood violates? Now whatever law of nature there is that the testimony's falsehood violates, that law must pertain to the testimony. But testimony pertains to a unique event—to a miracle. So within Hume's theory it does not make sense to speak of many occurrences with respect to the testimony. So it does not make sense to speak of a law of nature pertaining to the testimony. In that case, there is no law of nature that the testimony's falsehood violates. In that case, the testimony's falsehood cannot be miraculous. And if the testimony's falsehood cannot be miraculous, then the testimony's falsehood cannot be more miraculous then the event it is endeavoring to establish as miraculous. In that case, the supposition that underlies Hume's argument is empty. Now taking Hume's argument as an implication, the supposition that underlies the argument serves as the antecedent of the implication. So we can say that Hume's argument capitalizes on an empty (that is, false) antecedent. But there can be no valid argument that is based on the denial (that is, the falsity) of the antecedent. Therefore, Hume's argument is invalid.

Let us move on to Part II of Section X of Hume's Enquiry. Here in Part II Hume makes four points. The first point Hume makes has to do with the requirements that must be satisfied for a testimony about a miracle to be reliable. Hume's requirements are as follows: (1) there must be a sufficient number of people making the testimony; (2) the testifiers must be people of unquestioned good sense, education, and learning, such that there is a guarantee against delusion; (3) the testifiers must be of such integrity as to place them beyond all suspicion of trying to deceive others; (4) the testifiers must be of such credit and reputation in the eyes of mankind that they stand to lose a great deal in case of their being detected in any falsehood; and (5) the facts attested to must be performed "in such a public manner and in so celebrated a part of the world, as to render the detection unavoidable." Hume states that "in all history" these requirements have not been satisfied with any respect to any alleged miracle. That is to say, Hume believes that in all history there has never been a credible report of a miracle.

Now let us apply this to the resurrection of Jesus. Was there a sufficient number of testifiers? Yes, there was. Were the testifiers of such unquestioned good sense, education, and learning that we could be guaranteed against their being deluded? As for education, some of the testifiers were not educated. Paul, who became a convert after Christ had appeared to him on the road to Damascus, testified to the resurrection of Christ very strongly. And Paul was one of the most highly educated people of that day. But the fact that many of the testifiers were not educated people does not mean that they were deluded. After all, one does not have to be educated to see that Jesus died on the Cross. One does not have to be educated to see that the tomb was empty. One does not have to educated to see and hear Jesus in his post-resurrection appearances. After all, all it needed was good eyes and ears. The fact that many of the testifiers were not educated does not entail that they were deluded. The New Testament accounts of the resurrection do not provide any hint that the testifiers were deluded.

Did the testifiers have such undoubted integrity as to place them beyond suspicion of trying to deceive others? Yes, they were honorable people. Peter had told a lie earlier about his identity. But that was because he was afraid. But after the resurrection Peter was no longer afraid. He was the one who delivered the Pentecost message, in which he said to the men of Israel, 'This man [Jesus] was handed over to you by God's set purpose and foreknowledge; and you, with the help of wicked men, put him to death by nailing him to the cross.' Those are not the words of a man who was afraid. The coming of the Holy Spirit had transformed those simple folks into the bold testifiers that they were, pointing the accusing fingers to the enemies of Jesus, accusing them face to face of the crime of crucifying Jesus. Were the disciples deceivers? There is no indication at all. Had the disciples been deceiving the people, it would not have been difficult to prove their lie. If Jesus had not been raised, the religious leaders could have produced his body. The disciples could not have stolen the body of Jesus: the tomb was guarded. When the disciples went to the tomb on the morning of the third day they were surprised to see it empty. And when those who had gone to the tomb told the other disciples, these latter had a hard time believing. Thomas was very reluctant to believe.

Did the testifiers have a great deal to lose if their testimony was found to be false? Yes, indeed. They stood to lose their lives. The religious leaders did not like their testimony at all. They arrested the disciples, put them in prison. They were in constant danger. In fact some of them were killed.

Finally, were the facts of Jesus' death and post-resurrection appearances public? Very much so. Many people saw the crucifixion of Jesus. Many people saw Jesus in his post-resurrection appearances. At one time a crowd of five hundred saw the risen Christ. And the empty tomb stood there available for anyone to inspect.

We move on to the second point of Hume in Part II of his chapter on miracle. Hume says that in our reasonings we commonly go by the maxim which has the following elements: (1) unobserved objects resemble observed ones; (2) what has been found to be most usual is "always most probable"; (3) "where there is an opposition of arguments, we ought to give the preference to such as are founded on the greatest number of past observations." Then Hume says that although we normally proceed according to the above considerations, yet "when anything is affirmed utterly absurd and miraculous, it [the mind] rather the more readily admits of such a fact, upon account of that very circumstance, which ought to destroy all its authority. The passion of surprise and wonder, arising from miracles, being an agreeable emotion, gives a sensible tendency towards the belief of those events, from which it is derived" (p. 129). "A religionist may be an enthusiast, and imagine he sees what has no reality; he may know his narrative to be false, and yet persevere in it, with the best intentions in the world, for the sake of promoting a holy cause. . . " (p. 130). "The many instances of forged miracles . . . prove sufficiently the strong propensity of mankind to the extraordinary and the marvellous . . . " (p. 130).

Our response to the first part of the preceding point is this. We agree with Hume that in the normal course of things we go by the maxim he mentions; we assign a greater degree of probability to the more usual; the greater the evidence for something, the more we are inclined to believe it. And where there is what Hume calls "an opposition of arguments" we tend to assign a greater weight to that which has been confirmed by more past observations. Thus far we agree with Hume.

But since Hume means to use this maxim to rule out the possibility of miracles (we assume that that is his goal here), we object. Our objection is that in the case of miracles, which are unique events, we do not compare amounts of confirmatory data, we do not look for recurrence of similar data. The Humean notion of constant and regular conjunction does not apply to miracles—it can't, since miracles are nonrepeating phenomena. It does not make sense to speak of similar miracles; each miracle is unique.

Why do people believe in miracles? Hume says it is because of the influence of "the passion of surprise and wonder," which are agreeable emotions. Mankind, says Hume, "have a strong propensity to the extraordinary and the marvellous." In other words, belief in miracles is not an intellectual one; it is emotive. The tough-minded, Hume can be expected to say, will not believe in miracles because he uses his head instead of his emotions. It is people who are easily moved by their emotions who are inclined to believe in miracles.

Before we reply, let us present the rest of Hume's points. The third point Hume makes in Part II of his chapter on miracles continues the same emphasis on the lack of thinking on the part of miracle believers. "It forms a strong presumption against all supernatural and miraculous relations, that they are observed chiefly to abound among the ignorant and barbarous nations: or if a civilized people had even given admission to any of them, that people will be found to have received them from ignorant and barbarous ancestors ... " (p. 131). "... all proceeds from the usual propensity of mankind towards the marvelous ... " (P. 131). "It is strange ... that such prodigious events never happen in our days. But it is nothing strange, I hope, that men should lie in all ages" (p.132). [Hume's emphasis] "The advantages are so great, of starting an imposture among an ignorant people, that, even though the delusion would be too gross to impose on the generality of them ... it has a much better chance of succeeding in remote countries . . . The most ignorant and barbarous of these barbarians carry the report abroad" (p. 133). These remarks are punctuated by stories of miracle beliefs propagated among the ignorant and barbarous.

The fourth point made by Hume in Part II of Section X is that every testimony for a miracle is "opposed by an infinite number of witnesses; so that not only the miracle destroys the credit of testimony, but the testimony destroys itself" (p. 134). Here he gives several examples of miracle stories. Among the examples given is that of a Roman Catholic who had recovered a limb by rubbing holy oil on the stump. "This miracle was vouched by all the canons of the church; and the whole company in town were appealed to for a confirmation of the fact ... " (p. 137). Again here Hume talks about the "bigotry, ignorance, cunning, and roguery of a great part of mankind" (p. 137).

Thus Hume. Now we reply. First of all, we note the fact that most of the examples of miracles given by Hume are those believed by those he calls "ignorant and barbarous." Then he gives one example of a Roman Catholic who recovered his limb. The one thing Hume keeps hammering in this chapter is the ignorance, the barbarousness, the emotive tendency of those who believe in miracles. He states this point several times in different words in this chapter. For our reply, we make the following points. First, we agree with Hume that among the uncivilized many weird beliefs and practices prevail. The uncivilized, for example tribesmen living in remote jungles, are governed by their fear of the unknown. Their fear drives them to resort to all sorts of weird practices. On this matter we agree with Hume.

Secondly, we agree with Hume that even among the civilized there are people who tend to be influenced more by their emotions than by the mind. There are people who hold beliefs they are not even clear about. If you question their beliefs, they react emotionally. That we grant.

As our third response we state again that the issue between us and the unbeliever is the question of whether miracles are possible at all We hold that miracles are possible and that the miracles narrated in the Bible did take place; unbelievers, such as Hume, believe that miracles are practically impossible. And as far as the question of possibility is concerned, we need not defend all miracles; one example of a veridical miracle is sufficient to establish that miracles are possible. If X is practically impossible, then there cannot be a single occurrence of X. So in defending the practical possibility of miracles, we are NOT committing ourselves to defending all miracle stories; we are not obligated to defend all miracle reports. That is why we give only one example, namely, the resurrection of Christ. We need only one example of a miracle to establish our point that miracles are possible. We lay down the strong caution that miracle reports must be carefully investigated; we warn against easily believing each and every story. Hoaxes have been admitted after investigation. There can be hoaxes propagated for all sorts of reasons, propelled by all sorts of motives. Even today among civilized people the caution must be sounded that every miracle report must be carefully scrutinized. (The only miracles I am prepared to defend are the Bible miracles. And my defense would be based on the trustworthiness of the Bible documents.)

Our fourth point against Hume is this. It is extremely puzzling why in his entire chapter on miracles he does not refer to the Biblical miracles—not at all. That is very strange.

If Hume wanted to attack belief in miracles, he should have concentrated on the Bible miracles, since Christians believe them. But Hume does not devote even one sentence to the Bible miracles. Very, very strange indeed.

Our fifth point against Hume is that he ignores the fact that in the centuries of Christianity there have been many highly educated people who have believed the Bible miracles. Hume emphasized the tendency of mankind to be swayed by emotion and by wonder. That is true with some people who believe in miracles. But that certainly is not true of highly educated Bible believers. Hume must speak to the fact that many have come to believe the Bible in adult life, some becoming Christians after years of active unbelief. But Hume is completely silent on these facts.

So we conclude our study of Hume's attack on belief in the possibility of miracles. We have seen that Hume has failed to establish his point. As a radical empiricist, Hume should not rule out the possibility of unique phenomena happening. Observation can only report; it cannot legislate as to what can and what cannot happen. The language of can or cannot goes beyond the epistemological boundaries of observation. Hume fails to see the radical implication of his strong belief that all we can know of matters of fact we know by observation, and that all we can observe are loose and separate impressions. This indeed is very radical empiricism. It is a brand of empiricism that prevents Hume from precluding the (practical) possibility of unique events. True, Hume speaks a lot of laws of nature, but what he calls laws of nature are actually no more than observed patterns of constant and regular conjunctions of impressions.

If Hume is to rule out the possibility of miracles, he has to do a lot of repairing of his theory. But Hume died in 1776; he can no longer repair his theory.

Let us consider a contemporary opponent. One of the articles in the 1985 Encyclopedia of Unbelief("The Scientist as Unbeliever") was written by Dr. Isaac Asimov, Professor of Biochemistry at Boston University Medical School. Concerning the Bible miracles, Asimov has this to say: "The various 'miracles' of the Old and New Testaments, in which divine intervention suspended or subverted the operation of laws of nature, are not acceptable as part of the scientific universe, and there is no evidence outside the Bible that any of them actually took place." [2]

Asimov is saying three things here and we will respond to each of them. The first thing he says is that in the case of the Bible miracles God "suspended or subverted the operation of the laws of nature." Our reply is this. How does Asimov know that God suspended or subverted the laws of nature when He performed the Biblical miracles? Does Asimov know exactly how God brings about a miracle? For example, in the case of the resurrection of Jesus, the fact is that no one—not even the disciples closest to Jesus—knew how God raised Jesus. No one knew what happened in the tomb during the night. No one knew how Jesus regained life. No one knew how or at what time Jesus left the tomb. What the Bible tells us is that in the morning of the third day the tomb was found empty. What happened during the night? No one knew! Did God suspend the laws of nature? Who can answer that question? Exactly what God does when He performs a miracle no one knows. But that is not to say that He does not perform miracles or that He cannot. That is only to admit our ignorance as to how God performs miracles, what exactly He does.

I suspect that behind this idea of Asimov is the assumption that the laws of nature are inviolable so that nothing can happen unless it conforms to the laws of nature. Writes Asimov: "Science is based on certain assumptions, as all things must be. It assumes that the universe 'makes sense,' that it can be reasoned about, that the rules of logic hold" (p. 610). Asimov would say, I think, that if miracles are admitted then the universe would no longer "make sense," it no longer can be reasoned about, the rules of logic would no longer hold. Why not? Miracles do not disturb the ordinary course of nature. The fact that God raised Jesus from the dead did not change the fact that dead men remain dead. Miracles are, after all, unique phenomena; they do not disturb the order and the regularities in nature. God's changing water into wine at the

wedding in Cana did not change the properties of water in
other places. The only water affected by that miracle was the
water in the particular jars which Jesus had asked to be filled.
Water in other containers at that time retained their properties.
The course of nature was not affected. Asimov talks as if when
God performs a miracle the laws of nature are so altered that
the universe malfunctions; it does not. Miracles do not alter
regularities in the universe.

Should God will to perform a miracle, what is there to
prevent Him from doing so? The laws of nature? That would
put the physical universe above God in the sense that God
cannot do something that does not conform to laws of nature.
What is it about the universe that makes God unable to do what
He wills to accomplish in the universe? If from nothing and
simply by willing God could bring the universe into existence,
why can He not now bring about in the world something which
does not conform to the regularities observed by scientists in
the universe? Has the universe that God created become so
powerful that God the Creator and supreme Sovereign is
helpless in it?

Miracles, Asimov says, are not acceptable in "the scientific universe." I take it that by this Asimov means that in the
universe as known or knowable by science miracles are not
accepted. What does Asimov mean here? I think what he
means is something we have already mentioned earlier,
namely, that the scientist's adoption of empiricist methods
and criteria rules out the possibility of science's understanding the language of miracles. Our comment is: Of course.
Empiricist methods and criteria rule out as meaningless any
talk that involves God. And miracle talk essentially involves
God, since miracles are caused by God.

Another thing Asimov says in the quoted passage is that
outside the Bible there is no evidence that the Bible miracles
actually took place. Is he suggesting that because the evidence
is only in the Bible therefore the miracles did not happen?
Asimov's point must be that the Bible is not a reliable source
of information. We discuss the trustworthiness of the Bible in
chapter 6; the reader is referred to that chapter. The Bible

accounts of the death, burial, and post-resurrection appearances of Jesus are factual accounts; if Asimov wants to maintain that they are false accounts, then he must show that by means of a factual investigation. He cannot dismiss the New Testament accounts by means of just one sentence.

Our challenge to the unbeliever remains intact: he has to show that miracles cannot happen. Merely asserting that miracles have not happened or do not happen will not do. It has to be shown that miracles are impossible. Neither Hume nor Asimov has succeeded in showing that.

A. Wolf, professor of logic and scientific method, writes: "All scientific methods start from observed facts . . . ." [3] Now observation can only report what is observed; there is nothing in observation that dictates that this or that thing cannot happen. The laws of nature are no more than the regularities that scientists observe in the universe. Natural laws are not iron-clad, inviolable prescriptions. As Wolf puts it, "In its scientific sense the word 'law' means nothing more than a regularity or uniformity in the character or relation of certain classes of facts or events. It denotes just some intrinsic character, or mode of behavior, in certain classes of phenomena . . . ." [4] On the issue of whether miracles are possible, the one thing we want the unbeliever to do is to show what it is in the regularities observed in nature that precludes the possibility of something happening which does not conform to the observed regularities. This is the point we are insisting on. This is our challenge to the unbeliever.

Let us close this chapter by talking about the concept miracle and the question of whether empiricists can properly deny the occurrence of miracles. Empiricist unbelievers like Hume deny the occurrence of miracles. Can empiricists deny that miraculous events take place?

To answer this question we need to state the essential elements of the definition of "miracle." In the concept miracle there are two essential elements. One is the observable event that takes place in the world. The water in the jars became wine, had the taste of wine and not water. Paul heard a voice and saw a light; he lost his sight. All these are observable phenomena. The second essential element in the definition of "miracle" is the cause, namely, God. A miracle is an event caused by God. An event is not a miracle if it is not caused by God.

Can the empiricist deny that miracles occur? Our answer is no. The empiricist can deny that a given event occurred. For example, the empiricist can deny that the water in the jars at Cana tasted wine. And the disagreement at that point can be resolved by observation alone. To ascertain whether the water had become wine the procedure would be to conduct a chemical analysis to determine the properties of the liquid. All that is on the level of observation. As far as the occurrence in the world goes, both Christian and unbeliever resort to observation; as far as the space-time factors go, Christian and empiricist are on the same footing. It is logically proper for the empiricist to deny that the event in question occurred.

The big difference pertains to the second element of the concept miracle, the element of God as the cause of the miraculous event. This element, God, is unobservable since God is Spirit. The instruments of science cannot show any data corresponding to the name "God." In other words, as far as the empiricist is concerned, this element is meaningless. For the empiricist the word "God" is not a name; it is a word that does not point to anything at all.

Can the empiricist deny that miracles happen? He cannot. Why not? Because one cannot be properly said to deny that which is meaningless. Here is a sentence: "Yesterday John's uncle caught a five-foot yellow smell in the square round line." That's a grammatically correct sentence. Can you deny what it is saying? Can you affirm what it is saying? You cannot. Why not? Because it is not saying anything. There is nothing to affirm or deny. Suppose you meet a stranger on the road. As you approach each other, the stranger says to you, "No." You would think he was out of his mind. What was he saying no about? Since the concept miracle essentially involves God, and since God is Spirit and therefore in principle unobservable, therefore the empiricist cannot make sense of the concept miracle. For the empiricist there is no genuine concept miracle. There is only the word "miracle" but that word is meaningless. Therefore, strictly speaking the empiricist unbeliever cannot deny that miraculous events take place. All he can say is that talk about the occurrence of miracles is nonsense. Are miracles possible? The only answer open to empiricists is, "That question is meaningless." That is why we find it rather interesting that generally empiricist unbelievers deny the occurrence of miraculous events.

CHAPTER FOUR

GOD

4.1 CAN THE EXISTENCE OF GOD BE PROVED?

We often hear people, especially unbelievers, make the point that God's existence cannot be proved. Christians are often challenged to prove the existence of God. So it is important for us in this chapter on God to address the question directly: Can God's existence be proved? Now before we answer that question yes or no, it is in order first to make sure that we are clear as to what the question is asking. That is, we first must clarify the meaning of "prove."

The word "prove" or "proof" has its natural home in mathematics and in deductive logic. The strict, or primary, sense of "proof" is the one in mathematics and deductive logic. Sometimes the word "prove" or "proof" is used in what we may consider a secondary sense, in which the meaning is that of evidence, for example: "His frequent loss of memory is proof of his having many serious problems." Here "proof" has the meaning of "evidence." Now when it comes to the question of whether God's existence can be proved, it is clearly the primary, or strict, sense of "prove" that is intended. Those who have invented "proofs" for God's existence have invented arguments that are meant to lead <u>deductively</u> to the conclusion that God exists.

In deductive logic, a proof is a series of propositions (or statements) such that the initial proposition or propositions are "given" and the rest of the series are derived in a step-by-step manner from those that are given. The "givens" are usually called premises. A proof may have only one premise; it may have more than one. The truth of the premises is <u>assumed</u> in the proof; that is the point of calling the premises <u>given</u>. We can also think of the premises as the starting points of the proof. The most important thing about a proof that we must keep in mind is that the conclusion is <u>derived</u> from the premises in a <u>step-by-step</u> manner. Each step of the derivation must be justified by a rule of inference. It is because the conclusion is derived step by step from the premises that when we finally reach the conclusion, then if no mistake was made in the derivation, we can say that the conclusion <u>necessarily</u> follows from the premises. Another way of saying that is that if there has been no mistake in the derivation, any one who accepts the premises is <u>compelled</u> (by the rules of logic) to accept the conclusion.

Can the existence of God be proved? My answer is that so far no one has succeeded in <u>proving</u> that God exists. In a study I made of the arguments that have been called proofs of the existence of God, I came to the conclusion that not one of them succeeds; each one has at least one logical defect. I very much doubt that anyone can in the future come up with a proof of God's existence that has no logical difficulty. It is a well-known fact that the so-called proofs of God's existence are defective. Many have examined these proofs and found them unsuccessful.

Since our objective in this book is to defend the Christian faith, there is no need here to do a critique of the arguments that have been invented to prove God's existence. It is enough to state here that none of the so-called proofs that have been invented so far succeed in (deductively) establishing that God exists. The reader who wants to read the criticisms that have been made can easily find them in philosophical journals and books.

The reader might ask, "If no one has succeeded in proving that God exists, does that mean that there is no reason to believe that God exists?" Not at all. There are reasons. There are considerations that <u>converge</u> to make it <u>reasonable</u> to believe that God exists. I will call this approach to the question of God's existence the convergence approach. The considerations we will present converge to make belief in God's existence reasonable; the several considerations are meant to stand together as a group. Their combined force gives the believer the justification for his belief that God exists.

The considerations we will discuss here are not meant to be exhaustive; some people may be able to think of considerations which are not mentioned here. According to our convergence approach, whatever other considerations there may be beyond what we present below will just be added to the ones discussed here; the additional considerations increase the combined force of the convergence.

(1) As we will see in Chapter 6, the Bible is a trustworthy record of God's self-revelation. What the Christian finds in the Bible he takes to be history. Because of that, the entire Bible constitutes for the Christian the primary consideration that makes it reasonable to believe that God exists. The Bible focuses on God. The many miracles recorded in the Bible are ascribed to God. For example, it is written that it was God who raised Jesus from the grave. Now if God's existence is denied, it is impossible to make sense of the many miracles narrated in the Bible.

The Bible does not prove that God exists. The Bible assumes God's existence; nowhere does one find any attempt on the part of the Bible writers to prove that God exists. The Book of Genesis, the first book of the Old Testament, opens with the declaration that in the beginning God created the heavens and the earth (Gen.1:1). Nowhere does the Bible address the question of whether God exists. It was God who inspired the men who wrote what is now the Bible. So the very existence of the Bible is the primary consideration that makes it reasonable to believe that God exists.

(2) Of the many accounts one reads in the Bible, we want to single out for emphasis the story of the life, ministry, death, and resurrection of Jesus of Nazareth. Here was a man born to Mary before she knew any man. When this boy Jesus grew to be a thirty-year-old man he began telling people that he was

the Son of God, that he came from God, that God was his Father, that God and he were one. He told his close followers that he would be killed but that he would rise from the dead. He told them that he was returning to his Father and that he would return some day.

Jesus often spoke about God. One day he told a crowd of people that he and God are one (John 10:30). Philip, one of his followers, asked Jesus to show them the Father. Jesus asked Philip how it was that he (Jesus) had been with them so long and yet he (Philip) did not know him. Then Jesus made the startling claim that he who had seen him had seen God; so his followers should not have been asking him to show them the Father. He again declared that he was in the Father and the Father in him. He pointedly asked his followers if they believed that he was in the Father and the Father in him. He told them his words were really not his but those of the Father; he spoke not on his own authority. The Father did his work in Jesus. And he urged his disciples to believe that he was in the Father and the Father in him. He asked them to believe at least for the sake of the works. (John 14)

Of course he could have been out of his mind; he could have been simply a charlatan. But there was in Jesus' utterances and his actions a certain coherence that could not be ignored. Throughout Jesus' ministry his enemies could not find any trace of inconsistency in his utterances or any discrepancy between his utterances and his actions. And yet they were always trying to trap him. Each time that they put questions to him to trap him he always put them to silence. His character was very impressive. He had astounding powers. For example, he could tell what a man was thinking; that ability was demonstrated many times. Not only that, but this man Jesus healed many that were sick of different diseases. A woman who had had a blood flow for twelve years touched his garment and her blood flow stopped. Jesus healed the sick simply by saying certain words. He made blind persons see, lame ones walk. He even called Lazarus, who had been in the grave four days, to come out and Lazarus did come out.

Jesus had a certain aura of authority about him that even

his enemies recognized. One day he went to the temple and drove away those who were buying and selling, saying to them that 'my house' should be a house of prayer, but that the merchants had made it a den of robbers. (Luke 19:46)

He opposed the religious leaders of the Jews, who accused him of blasphemy for claiming to be one with God. Finally the religious leaders had him arrested, falsely tried and sentenced to death by crucifixion. Many saw him crucified. He died on the cross. During the time of his death there happened certain things that astounded the onlookers: "there was darkness over the whole land until the ninth hour, while the sun's light failed; and the curtain of the temple was torn in two." (Luke 23:44-45) Two friends buried him. His enemies wanted to make sure that his friends would not steal the body; so they asked for permission from the government to have the tomb guarded. Soldiers stood on guard outside the tomb.

But the morning of the third day the tomb was found empty. None of the guards saw any one leave the tomb.

After he had risen from the grave, Jesus appeared to his disciples during forty days; he spoke to them of the kingdom of God. (Acts 1:3) In his post-resurrection appearances Jesus was seen by other people. At one time he was seen by a crowd of five hundred. He sometimes would suddenly appear where his followers were and would talk with them. Then he would suddenly disappear. He said he was returning to his Father but promised that one day he will return. He commanded his followers to proclaim his message to the whole world. One day he disappeared from his followers and has not been seen bodily since then. Those who believe in him are expecting his return, the time of which he said no one knows except the Father.

The life, ministry, death and resurrection of Jesus is the most important of the considerations that converge to make it reasonable to believe that God exists.

Now we must point out to the unbeliever that the narrative of Jesus is a factual one. It is a historical account. If the unbeliever wishes to deny the historicity of Jesus, if he wishes to deny the occurrence of the events mentioned in the Biblical narratives on Jesus, he cannot do so simply by appealing to a theory or a criterion of meaning or knowledge. Questions of historicity cannot be resolved simply by appealing to a theory or a criterion. Data are logically prior to criterion or theory. This point is very important. If the unbeliever wishes to deny the story of Jesus, he must establish that the things stated in the story of Jesus did not happen. We maintain that the story of Jesus cannot be dismissed by simply saying that the events in the story of Jesus could not have taken place. "Could not" is the language of theory or of criterion; what we are dealing with here is a factual account. The unbeliever is reminded of the trustworthiness of the Bible (Chapter Six), in which we read the story of Jesus of Nazareth.

The Christian takes the story of Jesus as true. Since Jesus spoke of God many times the Christian believes that God exists. The fact that God was in Jesus is the most reasonable way of accounting for the astounding phenomena in the birth, life, death and resurrection of Jesus.

(3) Another consideration that makes it reasonable to believe that God exists is what happened to the close followers of Jesus after he left them. When Jesus was with his followers he told them that it was to their advantage if he went away, for if he did not go away the Holy Spirit would not come; but if he went away he would send the Holy Spirit to them. (John 16:7). When Jesus was about to leave them, after his resurrection, he told his close followers that they would receive power when the Holy Spirit had come upon them, and that they would be his witnesses in Jerusalem, in Judea, in Samaria, and to the end of the earth. (Acts 1:8)

In Chapter 2 of the Book of Acts we read that when the day of Pentecost had come, Jesus' followers were all together in one place. Suddenly they heard a sound from heaven; it sounded like a rushing mighty wind. The sound filled all the house in which they were sitting. They saw tongues of fire, resting on each of them. And they were filled with the Holy Spirit. They began speaking in other tongues, as the Holy Spirit gave them utterance. (Acts 2:1-4).

That unusual phenomenon was the turning point of the

careers of the close followers of Jesus. While they were with Jesus, in the last days, they were fearful people. When Jesus was arrested, Peter, who had professed loyalty to Jesus, denied him three times. He was asked if he was not one of Jesus' followers and each of the three times he said he did not know the man. When Jesus died, his close followers were afraid of the Jews. On the evening of that day, which was the first day of the week, the disciples had the doors shut. They were fearful for their lives, since they were closely identified with Jesus.

But after they had been filled with the Holy Spirit on the Day of Pentecost, they became totally different men. Peter, who because of fear had denied that he ever knew Jesus, stood before a large crowd on Pentecost Day and spoke very brave words about Jesus their risen Lord. Among other things, Peter told the crowd that Jesus had been crucified according to the definite plan and foreknowledge of God. He accused his audience of the crucifixion. But, said Peter, God raised Jesus up. (Acts 1:23) The speaker was certainly a very different Peter from the one who had earlier denied knowing his Lord. Face to face, Peter told the Jews that they crucified Jesus and killed him by the hands of lawless men. Strong language indeed.

What had happened to this man? What had caused the change? The one singular difference was that Peter, along with the other disciples, had been filled with the Holy Spirit. They had become transformed men. From that time on, the disciples kept on preaching Jesus; they kept telling people of the Son of God that had been raised by God from the dead. The opposition of the religious leaders of the Jews continued--of course. The disciples were persecuted. They were beaten, brought before tribunals, sent to prison, constantly threatened. But nothing could stop them. Told by the religious authorities to stop preaching Christ, Peter and John boldly declared that they would rather listen to God then to the religious authorities; they declared that they had to speak of what they had seen and heard.

This, we hold, is a strong consideration that helps to make

it reasonable to believe that God exists. Jesus said the Holy Spirit would come, that the disciples would have power when the Holy Spirit had come upon them. The promised Holy Spirit did come. And the disciples were transformed from fearful men to men who defied the very religious leaders who had sent Jesus to the Cross. Some of them were martyred because they would not stop talking about Jesus Christ. To us the change that had taken place in the lives of the close followers of Jesus is one of those considerations that <u>converge</u> to make it <u>reasonable</u> to believe that God does exist.

(4) Another consideration that reinforces our convergence argument is the experiences of Christians of God's working in their lives. We will discuss this point very briefly here since God-related experience is discussed at some length in Chapter 6. Throughout the two thousand years of Christianity there have been countless instances of believers experiencing answered prayer. A believer asks God to do something or to give something. His prayer is answered. It is then but reasonable that his belief in God's existence is strengthened. The fact that the atheist or the agnostic does not have any such experience proves nothing. It is quite unreasonable to argue that since the unbeliever does not have such experiences therefore there is no such thing as God answering prayer. That reasoning is quite unsound. That is reasoning from ignorance (<u>argumentum ad ignorantiam</u>)—which is fallacious. In the Bible there are stated and there are implied requirements for answered prayer. One of the stated requirements is faith. Without faith, it is said in the Bible, one cannot please God. Now the unbeliever does not believe in God, which means, of course, that he does not fulfill the requirements for answered prayer. In fact, the unbeliever does not pray. So naturally he does not experience answered prayer. But then his ignorance of answered prayer—of God working in his circumstances—does not constitute evidence that there is no such thing as the Christian's experience of God's working in his life.

(5) Another consideration that makes belief in God's existence reasonable is the existence of the universe. How do we account for the fact that this universe is here? How did the

universe come about? The theory of evolution cannot give a satisfactory answer to the question of the <u>origin</u> of the world since the theory of evolution <u>assumes</u> some material thing <u>already</u> in existence in the very beginning. The crucial question is: Where did the very first thing that was in existence come from? How did it come to be? The question of how <u>the very first thing</u> (whatever it was) came into being is different from the question of how things evolved. The Christian explanation is that in the beginning there was only God, eternal, all-powerful. And from nothing, simply by willing it, God brought the universe into being.

(6) There is also the fact that the universe is as orderly as it is. The view that God created the world out of nothing is the most satisfactory explanation of the fact of the orderliness of the universe. Now of course the orderliness of the universe does not constitute <u>proof</u> that God exists—recall our clarification of the use of the word "prove." The universe's orderliness is one of the considerations that make it reasonable to believe that God exists. As man marvels about the vastness and the orderliness of the universe, he cannot help wondering how it all came to be.

The preceding are considerations that <u>converge</u> to make it <u>reasonable</u> to believe that God exists. The considerations we have presented are not meant to be exhaustive. But we believe that they are sufficient to justify the Christian's belief in God's existence.

It is important to point out that our approach—the convergence approach—is not built on any assertion as to the nature of God. The question of what God is like—what God's attributes are—can come later. Our approach leaves open the question of what God's attributes are. The trouble with building the argument for God's existence on God's attributes (as is done by the ontological argument of Anselm) is that until we have established that God exists we are not yet in a position to say what God is like. Any claim to knowledge of God's attributes presupposes God's existence, since only what exists can have attributes. The question of what God's attributes are cannot properly be raised until <u>after</u> the question of God's existence has been dealt with. Our approach, the convergence approach, is not guilty of assuming any knowledge of God's attributes as a basis for arguing to God's existence.

4.2. OBJECTION: "HOW CAN YOU BELIEVE IN A GOD WHO WILLS THE KILLING OF PEOPLE? THAT CANNOT BE THE SAME AS THE GOD OF LOVE OF THE NEW TESTAMENT."

So goes the objection of some people. They point to places in the Old Testament where we are told either that God ordered the killing of men and women or that God enabled this or that Hebrew leader to defeat the enemy. One such passage is I Samuel 15:2-3, in which Samuel is quoted as telling King Saul that God was going to punish the Amalekites for opposing Israel when Israel was on the way to Canaan from Egypt. Samuel told Saul, upon God's instructions, to go and smite Amalek, and utterly destroy all that he (Amalek) had. The instruction was to destroy everything, including women and infants and animals.

Well, Saul did go and fight the Amalekites and defeated them. But he allowed the soldiers to keep the best of the animals; he did not kill Agag, the king of Amalek. When confronted by Samuel, Saul justified the action by saying that the soldiers were going to sacrifice the best animals to God at Gilgal. But God was displeased with Saul, who had been anointed king of Israel by Samuel at the order of God. Because of this disobedience, God rejected Saul as king. Now this would be one part of the Old Testament that these objectors would throw out as portraying a God different from the God of love of the New Testament.

Let us evaluate this reasoning. In the first place, there are in the Old Testament a good number of places in which Yahweh either ordered the extermination of people or enabled the Hebrews to defeat the enemy. These parts of the Old Testament were accepted by the early Christians and included in the canon. They have been accepted by the Christian community all theses centuries. The entire Old Testament as it now stands has been accepted by the Christian community as part of the Word of God, part of the inspired Scriptures. Let it be kept in mind that the Holy Spirit has been ministering to the Christian community all these centuries. In the Bible we find God ordering the killing of men, women, and cattle; but we also find a God who sent His only son to die for the sins of men. The sinless Son of God went through the agony of the Cross to save undeserving sinners. BOTH pictures of God are in the Bible—in the canon. BOTH portrayals of God have been accepted by the Christian Church all these centuries.

There is another consideration. By what criterion must these parts of the Old Testament be thrown out? What is the basis for deciding to keep the New Testament intact while throwing out some parts of the Old Testament? What is the criterion? What is the basis for that discrimination? This is an extremely important question. My strong suspicion is that the objector is setting up his own thinking as the basis, the criterion. The objector believes in a God of love but not in a God who orders the killing of people. Such a "contradiction" goes against the sense of propriety of the objector. "But how can God will the killing of people and at the same time be a loving God?" I do not know how, but He is such a God. The bottom line is that the entire Bible is the inspired Word of God, including the parts in which God ordered the killing of people or enabled Hebrew leaders to defeat enemies. What is involved here is fundamentally the question of authority, of basis. If we reject some parts of the Bible because we "cannot see how God can be such a contradiction," then we are making our own thinking the highest authority. We now set ourselves up as the supreme authority, so high that what the Spirit of God inspired to be written down we are willing to throw out.

Let us pursue this thought, this criterion. If we set up our own thinking as the highest authority, what is to prevent us from throwing out more parts of the Bible? Suppose some people throw out this or that book of the Old or the New Testament for this or that reason, what then? If we pursue the logic of this thinking, nothing can stop us from throwing out the whole Bible. Who is to tell me that I have no right to throw out whatever part of the Bible I feel must be rejected—if our thinking is to be the basis? My thinking must be as much authority as the thinking of anyone else, mustn't it?

God is the supreme sovereign. And that means that what God wills is authoritative in the highest sense. This affirmation is axiomatic. No matter how far we allow our minds to think we must never reach the point of thinking that we have the authority to "play games" with the absolute sovereignty of God. We must not allow ourselves to think that God's doings must somehow conform to our own thinking. We must not require of God that He conform to our own thinking. We must not require of God that He conform His decisions to our sense of right and wrong! No matter how much learning any man has acquired, God remains beyond his total comprehension. God's ways are far beyond our complete grasp.

If, as the Christian Church has affirmed all these centuries, the Scriptures are the inspired Word of God, then no matter how we feel or what we think about some parts of it, we are subject to the entire canonical Scriptures. That has been the testimony, the commitment, of the Christian Church all these centuries.

CHAPTER 5

CHRISTIAN FAITH

5.1 WHAT IS CHRISTIAN FAITH?

This simple-looking question can be complex in that the word "faith" has different uses. We speak of faith in the doctor who performs the delicate surgery. We speak of faith in the pilot who flies the plane across thousands of miles. There is faith in the future, as some people say. A young man in love marries his sweetheart; they have faith in each other. When the word "faith" is used in the religious domain, it can mean different things too. People speak of Mr. X's Moslem faith or of Mr. Y's Buddhist faith or of Mr. Z's Christian faith.

Regardless of what faith it is, faith is something internal. We might call it a state of mind; some people might prefer to say faith is a state of heart; some might prefer to say faith is a state of the heart and mind. Now insofar as faith is a state of mind, it is practically impossible to differentiate one faith from another since there is no way we can compare two states of mind and differentiate them. We are driven, then, to distinguish the different faiths from one another in some other way. The most fruitful way is differentiation on the basis of the object of faith. So we speak of faith in the pilot, faith in the doctor, faith in the postal service, faith in your husband or wife, the Buddhist faith, the Moslem faith, the Jewish faith, the Christian faith, and so on.

The twentieth-century philosopher Ludwig Wittgenstein

has left the world a very helpful idea. Wittgenstein said that there are many language-games each of which having its own rules. He warned that we must not impose the rules operative in one language-game upon another language-game, else we generate confusion. Wittgenstein stressed the importance of the <u>context</u> in which a word or sentence is used. He preferred speaking of the <u>use</u> of a word or a sentence to speaking of its <u>meaning</u>. The trouble with the idea of the meaning of a word is that people tend to think of words as carrying meanings as dogs carry tags. Wittgenstein insisted that words do not carry meanings wherever they occur; words, he maintained, are <u>used</u> differently in different contexts. The same word or sentence can be used to convey different ideas depending on how they are used. The word "faith" nicely illustrates Wittgenstein's point. We must insist on speaking of Christian faith instead of just faith, Since Christian faith is quite different from Moslem faith or Buddhist faith or faith in the pilot. In the Christian language-game the word "faith' means something quite different from what it means in other language-games. So in answering the question before us, we must speak of Christian faith.

What is Christian faith? The core of the concept Christian faith is Christ. Christian faith is belief in, commitment to, Jesus Christ. The story of Jesus Christ is told to you by someone, or you read the Bible. You learn that Jesus is the Son of God; that He was sent to earth to die for sinners; that He was hated by the religious leaders of the Jews; that they accused Him falsely before the political authorities of Palestine; that His enemies demanded that He be crucified, and that Pilate gave in to the people's demand; that He was crucified; that He died and was buried; that He appeared alive three days after His burial; that He was seen a number of times after His resurrection; that if you repent of your sins and put your faith in Christ, God will forgive your sins because Jesus had died for your sins; that eternal life is granted as a gift to those who put their faith in Christ. If, after learning all of that, you acknowledge your sins to God and receive Jesus Christ as your personal Savior and the Lord you want to follow, you <u>become</u>

a Christian. And you now have Christian faith. Becoming a Christian is a decision you make. Having made the decision to receive Christ as your Savior and Lord, then on the basis of what the Bible says, you now are sure that you will be with God eternally. That assurance is founded on the death and resurrection of Jesus Christ—not on any merit on your part. Eternal life is a gift from God given to all those who put their faith in Christ.

In the Biblical language-game, it is important to point out that faith is itself a gift from God. Isn't it such a marvelous thing that a sinner comes to confess his sins to God and asks Jesus Christ to come into his life? There have been thousands of stories of people who were deep in sin who came to Christ. "How did that happen?" That is the work of the Spirit of God. God draws a man to Christ. Of course one can resist God's drawing; many have done so and remained unsaved. But the point we are making is that those who do repent of their sins and receive Christ as Savior and Lord do so with God's help.

The intellectual element involved in faith is a necessary part; you can only believe what you understand. You cannot believe the Gospel unless you understand it. It is not intelligent to commit yourself to something you have not even understood. So the intellect is unavoidably involved in Christian faith. Belief in Christ follows understanding the Bible's plan of salvation.

Are we saying that one has to understand everything in the Bible before one can become a Christian? Not at all. It is enough to understand the basics that are involved in salvation. And you do not need a college degree to understand the Bible's plan of salvation. As for understanding everything in the Bible, theologians will tell you that they are still trying to understand many things in the Bible. The Christian's understanding of what the Bible says should continue growing year by year.

While we emphasize the role of the intellect, we must go on to put the greater emphasis on discipleship. The intellectual aspect of Christian faith is a necessary part, but it is the less important part.

The more important aspect of Christian faith is discipleship. Jesus calls people not only to put their faith in Him but—more importantly—to <u>follow</u> Him as Lord. In Jesus' utterances during his brief ministry, he laid a great deal of emphasis on discipleship. He taught this lesson in various ways. In one instance, Jesus told a group of Jews who had professed faith in him, 'If you continue in my word, you are truly my disciples, and you will know the truth, and the truth will make you free.' (John 8:31-32) It is very unfortunate that this utterance of Jesus has been very badly mishandled by many Christians; in my observation John 8:31-32 is the most often distorted passage in the entire Bible. I have heard and read it misquoted very many times. I have heard three preachers say in the sermon "You shall know the truth and the truth shall make you free." One of the three preachers had for his text (!) 'You shall know the truth and the truth shall make you free.' A university has written on the facade of its main building the words "Ye shall know the truth and the truth shall make you free." (What an irony; a university is supposed to be a place where truth and accuracy are given the highest priority. By writing in large letters on the facade of its main building a distortion of one of Jesus' utterances, that university is proclaiming a falsehood.)

In the Greek, the utterance of Jesus (John 8:31-32) is <u>conditional</u> in form. Now quoting Jesus' utterance as "You shall know the truth and the truth shall make you free' changes not only the intended meaning but also the intended emphasis of Jesus. We must respect the form of the Greek sentence. The form of a statement matters a whole lot as far as logic goes. Whether the clauses of a sentence are joined by "if then" or by "and" or by "or" or by "if and only if" makes a great deal of difference in logic. That is why we mention the fact that in the Greek, John 8:31-32 is conditional in form. We must heed that form or else we distort the statement very seriously.

If a statement is conditional in form, the if-part, the part that sets forth the condition, is the more important part of the statement. Let us take this example:

If you work three hours overtime tonight, you

may take tomorrow off.

Suppose you are a manager and you say that to an employee working under you. Suppose the employee does not work overtime that night but he takes off the following day and tells you that you had told him that he may take off that day. The employee can get penalized for that! Your statement was conditional in form. His taking off the following day was conditioned upon his working overtime three hours that night. Here we can see the tremendous importance of the if-part of a conditional statement. Here we see the seriousness of ignoring the if-part of a conditional statement.

Those who quote Jesus' utterance simply as 'You shall know the truth and the truth shall make you free' are like the employee who did not work overtime but who took off the following day! Surely the condition set forth was very important.

There is a rule of logic that can be used to demonstrate the seriousness of the distortion if Jesus' utterance is quoted the way it is quoted by so many Christians. But we will not go through the details of a logical demonstration. I think what has been said is enough to make the important point that since Jesus' utterance was conditional in form, then in quoting it it is extremely important to quote the if-part. To quote only the result-part of Jesus' conditional promise is to change both what Jesus meant and the emphasis he intended.

There is another rule of logic that can help us see why the distortion is very serious if we quote only the latter part of Jesus' utterance. Again we will not go into the details of the demonstration. It is enough for our purposes to show the result of applying this rule of logic. By applying this rule to John 8:31-32, we get the following three separate and independent conditional promises.

(1) 'If you continue in my word, you are truly my disciples.'

(2) 'If you continue in my word, you will know the truth.'

(3) 'If you continue in my word, the truth will make you free.'

These three separate conditional promises are <u>logically equivalent</u> to the one statement uttered by Jesus. In writing them separately we have not at all changed the meaning or the emphasis of Jesus. We have simply exhibited the logical structure of what Jesus said. Writing them separately helps to accent the importance of the conditional part of what Jesus said. Jesus gave those Jews who had expressed faith in him three <u>conditional</u> promises. In each of the three conditional sentences, a serious distortion results from omitting the conditional part. Both in terms of pure logic and in terms of the emphasis on discipleship that we see in the utterances of Jesus, it is a very serious distortion of what Jesus said to quote his utterance simply as 'You shall know the truth and the truth shall make you free.'

We have taken this time to discuss at least intuitively the logical aspect of Jesus' utterance in order to show how serious the distortion is when Jesus' utterance is quoted only as 'You shall know the truth and the truth shall make you free.' Very clearly Jesus meant to put the emphasis on the conditional part of his conditional promise.

Over and over again, in his teaching Jesus emphasized discipleship. To present Christian faith without the emphasis on discipleship is to misrepresent it. Christian faith has two essential ingredients: the intellectual ingredient and the discipleship ingredient. Discipleship has the greater weight.

Does this mean that the teaching of Jesus is to be "measured" by the lives of those who profess to be his followers? No, it does not. Jesus never indicated that the validity of his teaching depended on the performance of those who profess to be his followers. We must admit that side by side with Christians who sincerely, seriously endeavor to please God in their daily lives, there are people who profess to be believers in Christ whose lives do not show it. There are even those whose lives show the opposite. You do not have to look very far to find a professing Christian whose life is even worse than that of some unbelievers. But this fact does not invalidate Jesus' teachings. Why should it? Laws which are good do not become bad because there are people who violate them. Laws which are good remain good even if many people disregard them. Jesus prescribed the kind of life his disciples ought to live. Whoever puts his faith in Christ takes upon himself the lifelong obligation to live the Jesus way.

5.2 IS CHRISTIAN FAITH A LEAP IN THE DARK?

You often hear it said that Christian faith is a leap in the dark. Some Christians may have accepted that idea. Is it true? Before we answer the question, we need to ask what is meant by those who say that Christian faith is a leap in the dark.

(1) One possible meaning is that there are people who embrace Christian teachings without the benefit of intelligent inquiry. If you ask them to state the basis of their believing they cannot give a satisfactory account. Now is this true? Unfortunately it may be true that there are Christians that fall into this class. But their believing must be distinguished from Christian faith; that is, the essence of Christian faith must be distinguished from the faith of this or that man or woman, just as the essence of honesty must be differentiated from the honesty of this or that person. When we ask whether Christian faith is a leap in the dark, we are talking about the essence of Christian faith, not the faith of any particular person or group of persons. What it is to be a Christian, or what it is to believe in and be a follower of Christ is what our discussion must address.

Is it of the essence of Christian faith that it is embraced without evidence, without any basis or ground? The answer is clearly no. Indeed NO! Christian faith has a basis; it has ground; it has foundation. What is the foundation? The Holy Scriptures. The self-revelation of God recorded in the Bible— that is where the Christian system is founded upon. The entire architecture that is the Christian belief system is anchored on the story told in the Bible. Remove the Bible and you have removed the entire foundation of Christian faith. As the apostle Paul puts it in his letter to the Romans: "For I am not ashamed of the gospel: it is the power of God for salvation to every one who has faith, to the Jew first and also to the Greek.

For in it the righteousness of God is revealed through faith for faith . . ." (Rom. 1:16-17). Little wonder that when he departed from the apostles Jesus specifically commanded them to preach the gospel to the whole world. Since the days of Paul to our day many Christians have devoted their lives to the great task of telling people of Jesus Christ. Whether it is in large meetings or in quiet one-on-one conversation, whether it is by speaking or by means of books or articles, the gospel of Jesus Christ continues to be communicated. And sinners continue to repent of their sins and to put their faith in Jesus Christ. Christians have a message, a very definite message: the gospel. The unbeliever is invited to open the pages of the Holy Scriptures and to read them with an open mind. They, the Scriptures, are the foundation of Christian faith. No, Christian faith is not a leap in the dark!

(2) Another possible meaning of those who say that Christian faith is a leap in the dark is that Christians use reason as far as they can and when they can no longer do so they just accept blindly whatever there is to be believed. Is this true of the essence of Christian faith? No, it is not. Some may proceed in that way but that is not of the essence of Christian faith. As indicated earlier, it is on the basis of what the Bible says that one becomes a Christian. There is nothing blind about Christian believing; there is no irresponsible jumping off without using one's head. In reading the Bible, one has to use his intellect. One must grasp certain Bible truths before he becomes a Christian. Throughout, one's reasoning power ought to be at work.

(3) A third possible meaning of those who say that Christian faith is a leap in the dark is that there are things that the Christian believes (for example, that there is life after death) that he really does not and cannot know. Is this true of the essence of Christian faith? Yes, it is. The writer of the book of Hebrews puts it this way: "Now faith is the assurance of things hoped for, the conviction of things not seen." (Heb. 11:1) The sinner who has received Christ as his personal Savior and Lord looks forward to eternal life with God; he believes that the grave is not his end. But he does not and

cannot know that there is life beyond the grave; he believes it. That is part of the meaning of Christian faith. But is that blind believing? No. Blind believing means, it seems to me, believing that has no foundation. The belief in eternal life is based on the belief in the divinity of Jesus Christ and the fact that Jesus Christ died to make eternal life possible for those who put their trust in Him. The belief in the divinity of Jesus and in the integrity of the claims of Jesus is grounded on the birth, life, ministry, death and resurrection of Jesus; there is solid ground for the faith. The Bible states that those who put their faith in Christ will have life everlasting. The Christian bets his life on that promise because of who Jesus is. He is not leaping in the dark. The future is not dark as far as the Christian is concerned; the future is in God's hands.

As far as that goes, if we say that a belief that counts on things that are yet future (and hence unknown) is a leap in the dark, then all people, believers and unbelievers alike, believe very many things by doing a leap in the dark. Let us consider just two examples. (1) You believe that tomorrow the sun will come up in the same direction from where you live. Do you know that? Strictly speaking, you do not know it. But you believe it. (2) Here are two young persons who are in love with each other. They think they know each other enough. They decide to get married. Do they know that they will be faithful to each other? They really do not know that; they believe it. Their belief that each of them will remain loving and lovable is based on what thus far they know of each other. Now if that is leaping in the dark, then we have to say that in very many instances people make leaps in the dark in believing this and that. The point that must be emphasized is that the real test of reliability of your "leap" is the basis on which the leap is made. Two persons who get married base their belief that their future will be good on what they know of each other. And they are human beings. Now the Christian's belief in such matters as life after death is based, not on the integrity of human beings, but on the integrity of Jesus Christ the Son of God. And that makes all the difference.

5.3 IS CHRISTIAN BELIEF RATIONAL?

The reader may want to express this question as: Is Christianity rational? Both expressions come to the same thing. Now before we attempt an answer, the key word "rational" must be clarified.

In Webster's New Twentieth Century Dictionary "rational" is given four meanings, namely: (1) "of, based on, or derived from reasoning"; (2) "able to reason; reasoning; as, an infant is not yet rational"; (3) "showing reason; not foolish or silly; sensible; as, a rational argument"; (4) in mathematics, designating a number or quantity expressible without a radical sign as an integer or as a quotient or an integer." Which meaning of "rational" does the questioner have in mind? Obviously it is not the meaning in mathematics. Neither does the questioner mean to speak of the ability to reason, since Christian belief, or Christianity, cannot be spoken of as having or lacking some ability. It seems, then, that the first and the third of the meanings listed by Webster state what the question contemplates. In other words, probably the questioner is asking either or both of two questions: (1) whether Christianity is sensible, not foolish or silly; or (2) whether Christianity is based on, or derived from, reason. Let us answer the question by addressing these two resulting questions.

(1) Is Christianity, or Christian belief, sensible, not foolish or silly? That is, are there reasons for believing in Christianity? Can a reasonable person believe in Christianity? Clearly, the answer is a strong yes. Christian beliefs can be discussed, argued about; they can be explained, accounted for. If to believe foolishly or sillily is to believe without any reasons, then Christian belief is definitely not foolish or silly believing. The Christian who understands his faith is not averse to reasoning things out when it comes to his faith. Indeed he is enjoined by the Bible to be prepared to give a defense for the hope that he holds: "Always be prepared to make a defense to any one who calls you to account for the hope that is in you . . . ." (I Peter 3:15). The Biblical system can stand reasoned scrutiny; the Christian ought not to shy

away from a critical examination of his beliefs. Being prepared to give an answer to someone who asks about the Christian faith is a Christian's obligation and privilege.

Unfortunately, Christians sometimes talk as if Christian belief had no foundation. Some people even say that in Christian believing you believe what you do not understand. Which is impossible. How can you believe what you have not even understood? Suppose I give you this sentence: "The young lion's dream last night smelled sixteen kilometers per pound." Can you tell <u>what</u> this sentence is saying? Of course not. It is not saying anything; there is nothing to believe.

The sentences of the Christian religion are not nonsensical sentences; they express definite propositions. The Christian believes what he has understood, as anyone else who believes anything does. Further, the ideas in the Christian system are so related to each other that it is possible for the Christian to give reasons for what he believes.

That is not all; the Christian system is not a mere group of ideas floating without any kind of support outside of itself; it is no mere formal system with no connection to reality. The fact is that the real foundation of Christianity is reality—phenomena, events. The Christian religion is a history-grounded religion. That history is told in the Bible. One cannot be said to know what Christianity is until he has seriously considered what is written in the Bible.

(2) It is time now to consider the second subquestion. Is Christianity based on, derived from, reason? The answer is an emphatic no. If you say that Christianity is based on, or derived from, reason, you are saying that the intellect of man is the origin, the <u>foundation</u>, of the Christian religion. Nothing can be farther from the truth! To say that is to totally misunderstand Christianity. As we have stated earlier, the foundation, the basis, of Christian faith is reality, events—history. The Christian makes use of his ability to reason, yes; he makes use of his intellect as he seeks to understand what the Bible says, as he seeks to give reasons for his faith. But to make use of the intellect thus is entirely different from <u>deriving</u> Christianity from the intellect. The intellect, or rea-

son, is no more than man's capacity to perform certain logical functions, the ability to see relationships among things or ideas. The scientist uses his reason in making judgments concerning the data he has gathered. But the reality that the scientist reasons about is not <u>derived</u> from his intellect!

5.4 IS IT INTELLIGENT TO BELIEVE IN GOD?

At one time I was in conversation with several other persons; we were talking about the Bible. At one point one of us said that his wife would not believe the Bible "because she is very intelligent." Did he mean that intelligent persons do not believe the Bible? Did he mean that to believe in God is <u>the same thing</u> as being not intelligent? That is, did he mean "intelligent" = "does not believe in God," or: "believe in God" = "not intelligent"?

This must be the idea behind the following statements of Nietzsche: "Let us make no mistake—great minds are skeptical. . . . . The strength and the freedom which arise from exceptional power of thought express themselves in skepticism. . . . A mind which aspires to great things and is determined to achieve them is <u>of necessity</u> skeptical."[1] (Emphasis mine) Here Nietzsche makes a blanket assertion—a universal statement: great minds are skeptical. How shall we take this statement? Either we take it as saying that <u>without a single exception</u> great minds are skeptical (= great minds do not believe in God), or we take it as saying that with some exceptions great minds do not believe in God. How did Nietzsche take it? Most probably Nietzsche took this statement to be universal, that is he probably took it to mean that in every single case great minds do not believe in God. If we take this assertion to be universal, then we need only one exception to make it false. Logic requires that if an affirmative statement is universal, then one negative instance is sufficient to falsify it.

We can point to many great minds who believed in God. The mathematician and philosopher Descartes believed in God. Descartes even had his version of the ontological argument for God's existence. The mathematician Blaise

Pascal believed in God. C. S. Lewis, professor at Cambridge University, became a Christian late in life. In his book The Recovery of Belief (1952) , the English philosopher Cyril E. M. Joad writes: "Until comparatively late in my life the deliverances of reason no less than the weight of the evidence seemed to me to tell heavily against the religious view of the universe . . . ."[2]

Now would Nietzche say that these men we have mentioned were not great minds? Surely not. But if Nietzche would admit that the philosopher Cyril Joad, the literature professor C. S. Lewis, the mathematician-philosopher Descartes, and the mathematician Pascal were great minds—if Nietzche admits that, then what happens to his statement that great minds do not believe in God? In fact, in the past two thousand years there have been very many great minds who have believed in God. Today there are great minds who believe in God. Of course there also have been great minds who have not believed in God—we are not denying that. What we are questioning is the generalization of Nietzche that great minds do not believe in God. That is simply false. A universalized statement, such as "All great minds do not believe in God," is made false by just one exception. But in this case we find very many exceptions.

In the case of those who do not believe in God, is it the greatness of their minds that makes them unbelievers? If the answer is yes, then what are we to think in the case of those who are great minds but who believe in God?

If it is insisted on that to believe in God is to be not intelligent, then what we have is not a generalization but a definition! The story has been changed very much. A definition is not a statement capable of being true or false; a definition is not meant to make an assertion. A definition is meant only to tell us how a certain linguistic expression is to be used. Now as far as making or giving definitions goes, anyone can invent any definition he likes. But nothing happens to reality by virtue of the fact that someone has proposed a certain definition.

The trouble with the definition "great mind" = "a person

who does not believe in God" is that it rubs against common usage. Communication demands that we take common usage very seriously. And should we wish to use a familiar word in a special way—perhaps for some special purpose—then we have to tell our readers or audience that we are giving the word in question a special use, else we generate confusion.

I assume that our understanding of the use of the word "intelligent" coincides with the common usage. Now I take it that by the common understanding of the word "intelligent" it cannot be said that those who believe in God are necessarily (by definition!) not intelligent or less than intelligent. Common usage has it that there are great minds who believe in God, and there are great minds who do not. Simply from the fact that a person is a great mind we cannot know whether that person believes in God or not.

5.5 IS CHRISTIAN FAITH KNOWLEDGE?

This is an important but difficult question. The reason it is difficult is that the question of what knowledge is is far from easy to deal with. Since Plato to this day the philosophers have been debating the question of what knowledge is, or what it is to know. The debate among philosophers still goes on today; more and more detailed issues have been brought into the discussion. Theories have been advanced and attacked. Some theories have been abandoned or modified. Some individual philosophers have changed positions in the course of their philosophical careers.

The central point of controversy in the philosophers' debate on what it is to know has to do with criteria for determining the adequacy of reasons for claiming knowledge. When it comes to what David Hume calls matters of ideas, such as propositions in mathematics or other purely symbolic systems, agreement has been easier to come by, although even here there is no unanimity of opinion among philosophers. Kant's notion of synthetic a priori differs from the majority view on ideas which are not dependent on experience. The really knotty problems have to do with matters of fact, matters having to do with reality, with what is out there. It is in this area that the philosophical debate on what knowledge is continues to be hot.

My problem in dealing with the question of whether Christian faith is the same thing as knowledge is that in writing this book I am not assuming that the reader has taken courses in philosophy. Neither am I assuming that the Christian who reads this book has read books on philosophical theology. This book is intended for the general Christian community.

Should we at all enter into even a simplified specimen of the philosophical debate on what it is to know? The trouble is that even a supposedly simple handling of the issues surrounding the question what knowledge is is complicated. A presentation that is too sketchy not only is not helpful but also can be misleading. So perhaps it is best not to enter into the philosophers' debate of what knowledge is.

All we will say here is the following. Both philosophers and non-philosophers do distinguish belief from knowledge. Even in ordinary discourse we do demand a lot more of the person who claims that he knows something than of one who merely says he believes something. A person who says he believes that such and such is the case does not have to give us reasons for his belief; he may if he wants to, but we do not count him as under obligation to give reasons for his belief. It is not odd for a person to say, " I believe that such and such, but I have no reasons for my belief." Of course his belief would carry more weight if he supports it with reasons; but it is not necessary to support a belief with reasons. But he who claims to know something is under obligation to give reasons for his claim. If he refuses to give a reason or says he cannot give a reason, we then think his claim to knowledge does not have to be taken seriously. More importantly, the reasons given must be acceptable to us. If we think that his reasons are not reasonable, not acceptable, we withhold our assent to his claim to knowledge.

And that is where the question of whether Christian faith is the same thing as knowledge becomes quite important. The key problem is: What reasons are reasonable, or acceptable?

What are the criteria for determining which reasons are reasonable, which reasons are acceptable? Acceptable by whom? Who determines the criteria? Should the vote of any person have as much weight as the vote of any other? If not, why not? And if the vote of each person must have the same weight as the vote of any other, then what if many persons do not agree as to whether a given claim to knowledge is warranted or not? Further, if the criteria are taken from a certain discipline or subject matter, must the Christian accept those criteria? If the Christian must accept the criteria offered, why must he? If not, why not? These are extremely important questions.

Moreover—and for the Christian this is very important— must the Christian subject matter be lumped in the same basket as science and other secular subject matters? Or must the Christian subject matter be treated as unique, as a class by itself, and hence not subject to the criteria that may be workable with respect to other subject matters? In Wittgenstein's very useful notion of language-game, each language-game has its own rules of operation, its own criteria. The rules and criteria operative in one language-game must not be imposed on other language-games, else confusion arises. In line with Wittgenstein's concept of language-game, we can reasonably maintain that the Christian language-game can have its own use of the word "know"; and the Christian use of "know" must not be subjected to the criteria of knowledge adopted in philosophical or scientific contexts. After all, the Christian language-game is no less legitimate as a language-game than any other. Or, in any case, the question of the legitimacy of the Christian language-game cannot be answered by appealing to rules or criteria operative in secular language-games; that move would constitute imposing the rules/criteria of one language-game on other language-game— and that is illegitimate.

Having made some general remarks, let us now address directly the question before us: Is Christian faith knowledge? If we consult a concordance, we find that the verb "know" occurs in very many sentences in the Bible. The question is:

Does the Bible use the verb "know" in the same way scientists and philosophers use it? Should the criteria for knowledge used in science or philosophy—or in secular ordinary discourse—be applied to the Bible's use of the verb "know" or the noun "knowledge"? This is a very important question. An examination of the occurrences of "know" or "knowledge" in the Bible shows that in some cases "know" is used in the way it is used in secular contexts but that in the great majority of cases "know" is used differently from the way it is used in the secular contexts. In other words, in some cases we can apply the criteria for knowledge used in science or philosophy to the Biblical use of "know," but in the majority of cases the secular criteria for knowledge do not apply to the Biblical use. In the Christian language-game, for the most part "know" has a different use; it can be taken as involving faith.

To make the point clearer, let us consider some examples. In the gospel of John chapter 6 we read that there were Jews that murmured because Jesus had said that he was the bread from heaven. They asked themselves whether Jesus was not the son of Joseph, "whose father and mother we know." Those Jews knew the parents of Jesus and the parents of Joseph. They knew them in the same way that we know our friends or neighbors. This use of "know" is no different from the use of "know" in secular discourse, whether in ordinary discourse or in science or philosophy. The secular criteria for knowledge apply to this use of "know".

But this use of "know" is not the usual use in the Bible. In the great majority of cases, the Biblical use of "know" is very different. Let us look at just two examples of the peculiar Biblical use of "know." In the first epistle of John, we read this: "And this is the confidence which we have in him, that if we ask anything according to his [God's] will he hears us. And if we know that he hears us in whatever we ask, we know that we have obtained the requests made of him." (I John 5:14-15) In this passage, the use of "know" is quite different from the use of "know" in science or philosophy. Here "know" involves faith. If to these occurrences of "know" we apply the criteria for knowledge used in the secular context, the word "know" is misused. In this passage, so much is assumed about God; verse 15 is meaningful only in the context of faith. Remove faith, remove God, and verse 15 is meaningless. In this passage, the word "know" is practically synonymous with "have faith." In other words, in this passage "knowledge" is practically synonymous with "faith." And this is the typical Biblical use of the verb "know."

Here is another example. In the second letter of Paul to the Corinthians, we read this: "For we know that if the earthly tent we live in is destroyed, we have a building from God, a house not made with hands, eternal in the heavens." (II Cor. 5:1) If you show this sentence to the agnostic or atheist scientist or philosopher, he cannot make any sense of it. The verb "know" as used here means nothing to the unbeliever. By his criteria for knowledge, the verb "know" is misused in this passage. But is it misused? Not if we have the Bible context in mind. Not if we see the verb "know" as playing a role in the Christian language-game. Here we have an expression of faith, the faith of the Christian that the grave is not the end, that there is life with God, eternal life. Here, again, we see the verb "know" used as meaning "have faith." What this verse is saying is that we have faith that there is eternal life with God.

The reader might ask, "Is it legitimate to have a different use of "know" than that in science or philosophy?" Why not? There is nothing wrong with using the word "know" in a way different from the way it is used in science or philosophy—or in secular ordinary discourse. Words are used to talk about experiences and the things we deal with in daily life. Now life is much larger than science or philosophy or secular life. The Christian life is one form of life actually lived by millions of people in all parts of the world. The language of science or philosophy is unable to express many things that are very real in the religious commitment and experiences of Christians. Why should Christians be deprived of a language that fits their lives as Christians? Why, for example, should Christians be limited to the use of "know" in science or philosophy? As long as we do not mix uses of "know" there should be no problem having the word "know" in the Christian language-game. We get confused if we impose the use of "know" in the language-game of science or philosophy on the Christian language-game, or vice versa. As long as we observe the peculiarities of each language-game, there should be no trouble.

5.6 IS REVELATION BELIEVABLE?

Christianity is a revelation-grounded religion. The central affirmation of Christianity is that God, the one God who created the universe, made Himself known to man in various ways. As the writer of the book of Hebrews puts it: "In many and various ways God spoke of old to our fathers by the prophets, but in these last days he has spoken to us by a Son, whom he appointed the heir of all things, through whom also he created the world. He [i.e., Jesus] reflects the glory of God and bears the very stamp of his nature, upholding the universe by his word of power." (Hebrews 1:1-3) The Bible tells the story of God's self-disclosure. In this sense, Christianity is unique; it is the only religion whose central affirmation is that God revealed Himself, through the prophets and most prominently in Jesus. The Bible declares that God came to earth in and through Jesus, born of a virgin. Jesus, the Bible says, is the image of the invisible God. In these affirmations, Christianity is unique; no other religion makes these affirmations.

But the unbeliever can hardly wait to raise his objections. It is not surprising that he does. To the unbeliever who evaluates statements by the (empiricist) criteria of science all this talk about God disclosing Himself is sheer nonsense. It is plain foolishness. In fact, the Bible says precisely that. "The unspiritual man does not receive the gifts of the Spirit of God, for they are folly to him . . . ." (I Cor. 2:14) Why would a person who adheres to the criteria of science think that talk about revelation is nonsense? The answer is simple. Science bases its judgments on observation—on what can be gotten at by means of the senses (the use of instruments assumed always). If you talk about anything which cannot be known by using the techniques of science, then what you are saying is not verifiable even in principle. So it is nonsense. Now here's this talk about revelation. How do we go about using the techniques of science checking out the claim that God has made Himself known? What kind of evidence will confirm or disconfirm the claim that God has revealed Himself? The empiricist is completely at a loss. So his conclusion is that the Christian's talk about revelation is meaningless. And he is right—from his point of view.

The Christian's response is: Of Course! If you require that the Christian's talk about God's self-disclosure be subjected to the criteria of science, then of course the Christian's talk is meaningless. But why must the Christian's statements be evaluated in terms of the criteria of science? The Christian agrees that as far as knowing about the universe is concerned the method and criteria of science are the best, the most efficient man has come by. But why must the method that suits research into natural phenomena be applied to talk about God? God is Spirit, God is categorially different from natural phenomena. Why must the methodology that works well with natural phenomena be imposed on God-talk? This is the sixty-four-dollar question. Theology is a subject matter totally different from physics or biology or any other natural science. God-talk has its own logic. And that logic is unique. The logic of God-talk stands side by side with the logic of science-talk. It is illegitimate to insist that God-talk be subjected to the requirements or the criteria of science-talk.

In the first letter of the apostle Paul to the Corinthians we read, ". . . no one comprehends the thoughts of God except the Spirit of God. Now we have received not the spirit of the world, but the Spirit which is from God, that we might understand the gifts bestowed on us by God." (I Cor. 2:11b-12) The Spirit of God indwells those who have received Christ as personal Savior. This is what Paul means when he says "we have received . . . the Spirit which is from God." (The "we" he is speaking about is himself and the Christians of Corinth he was writing to.) Humanity can be divided into two groups: those who have the Spirit of God and those who don't, or those who are spiritual and those who are natural. Now it is only the Spirit of God who understands the thoughts of God; it is the spiritual man who can understand things about God. The natural man cannot understand things related to God, since such things are spiritually discerned. A brilliant scientist or philosopher who does not have the Spirit of God cannot understand, much less appreciate, things related to God. That is why the natural man is not in a position to judge as to whether revelation is believable or not. If you ask the natural man whether God has revealed Himself to the world, he will not be able to say anything except perhaps to say that he cannot make any sense of what you are saying. He is not in a position to deny that God has revealed Himself; denial implies that one understands what one is denying. The correct thing for the natural man to say is that he cannot make sense of talk about revelation. But to those who have the Spirit of God, revelation is not only believable; it is a foundation datum. There are Christians because God has revealed Himself and because there are people who have put their faith in Christ.

100

CHAPTER SIX

THE BIBLE

6.1. THE AUTHORITY OF THE BIBLE

During the discussion time following a lecture I gave on miracles at a church a lady made the comment that what I had said was all right if we accept the Bible as authoritative. I told her that her question was quite in order and important, that in a discussion such as the one we were having the Bible's authority was assumed.

I was impressed by the fact that that lady was led to ask that question in the course of our discussion about miracles; her asking the question called my attention, again, to the centrality and importance of the issue of the Bible's authority.

Why is the question of the Bible's authority important? One reason is that one of the prime targets of unbelievers' attacks is the Bible. As we mentioned earlier (see 1.1) the Academy of Humanism, an international association of scholars, has launched a project to discredit the Bible. And that is understandable, since the Bible is the intellectual base of Christianity. If the unbeliever succeeds in discrediting the Bible, then he has completely discredited Christianity. As long as the Bible stands, the unbeliever has a big problem.

A second reason why the question of the Bible's authority is important is that Christians appeal to the Bible to justify their beliefs and practices. If one's thinking and acting are based on a book, then one needs to know if that book is authoritative and if so why. For those Christians for whom the Bible is just a book that gathers dust on the shelf, well, the question of the Bible's authority is not anything to bother about. But for Christians for whom the Bible is the standard of faith and practice, for Christians who make small and big decisions in all areas of their lives on the basis of what the Bible says, the question of the Bible's authority is very important indeed.

A third reason why we need to emphasize the authority of the Bible is that the Bible is not the only book that people consider sacred. Other religions have their own sacred books. More importantly, the various sacred books of the different religions do not agree on many points, some of which are so fundamental that it is logically impossible for a person to subscribe to any two of the sacred books without seriously contradicting himself. The fact is, of course, that the adherents of each religion believe that their book is the true one. But since the different sacred books disagree on many points, some of them fundamental points, logic prevents any two of them from being true together. When A, B, C are contrary to each other, either all of them are false or only one of them is true. For example:

(1) The tallest buildings in the world are in New York City.

(2) The tallest buildings in the world are in London.

(3) The tallest buildings in the world are in Singapore.

These statements are contrary to one another. They can all be false but they cannot all be true; in fact, no two of them can be true. It happens that (1) is true, which means that the other two are false.

If A and B contradict each other on a given point, if A is true then B is necessarily false; if B is true, then A is necessarily false. For example:

(4) All men die.

(5) Some men do not die.

These two statements contradict each other. If (4) is true, then (5) is necessarily false; if (4) is false, then (5) is necessarily true.

The rules of logic make it necessary to inquire into the truth status of the sacred books of the different religions. Since the different religions cannot all be true, since it is logically impossible for a person to believe any two of the different religions without contradicting himself, then the adherents of each religion should be concerned about the truth status of their religion. For Christians, inquiry into the question of the authority of the Bible is very important.

And so we ask: On what is the authority of the Bible based? But before we address this question, let us first make a distinction that should be helpful in our dealing with this question. A distinction must be made between the order of reality and the order of knowledge. The order of reality logically precedes the order of knowing. That is, we can know only what is there. But what is there can be there without anyone knowing or believing that it is there. The fact that no one knows or believes that X is there does not diminish one whit the fact that X is there. Thomas Gray's poem "An Elegy Written in a Country Churchyard" is helpful here. In this poem Gray writes: "Full many a gem of purest ray serene the dark unfathomed caves of ocean bear; full many a flower is born to blush unseen, and waste its sweetness on the desert air." There are many beautiful flowers that no human eyes see because they are out there where human beings normally do not go. Some of those flowers could be more beautiful than many flowers that men and women have seen and considered beautiful. And there are gems lying deep in the ocean which no man will ever see. The point is that something can be there without anyone knowing that it is there. Something can have a certain quality without anyone discovering that it has that quality.

If the Bible is the Word of God, its being the Word of God belongs to the order of reality, whereas its being known to be the Word of God belongs to the order of knowledge. If (contrary to fact) no one had known or believed that the Bible is the written Word of God, the Bible would still have been the written Word of God. In other words, the Bible's being the Word of God is not dependent on that fact's being known or believed by anyone.

Now let us address the question before us. Why do Christians take the Bible as authoritative? The most important reason is Jesus' attitude toward the Bible. This statement is grounded on the fact that Jesus of Nazareth was no mere human being, no mere great teacher. Jesus is the Son of God. Since Jesus is the Son of God, his view of Scripture is most to be trusted.

We can hear the unbeliever objecting, "But that is <u>argumtum ad verecundiam</u>" (arguing "from authority"). <u>Argumentum ad verecundiam</u> is classified in logic textbooks as a fallacy. And we can see why it is a fallacy. The idea is that a statement is not true simply because it is uttered by some particular person; a statement is true because what it states is so. It is the same with arguments. An argument is valid if every step conforms to the rules of inference, not because it is believed by some particular person. We do recognize the soundness of that principle.

But in actual life we very often do appeal to authority, don't we? We hear someone say, "C'mon, why listen to him, what does he know about fishing?" Or: "You should have heard Mr. X's lecture at the Auditorium last night; that man's words carry so much weight. He knows what he's talking about." It is a well-known fact that we do recognize certain persons as having greater authority on some things than others. The professor spent years getting his advanced training in his field of specialty. Now as a professor, he continues to study his special area. The professor writes articles or books in his specialty. So when it come to his specialty, we look up to him. The idea behind looking up to an authority is that because of his special qualifications on the subject the judgments he makes on matters pertaining to that subject are <u>more likely</u> to be true than the judgments of someone who does not have his qualifications in that area. What the fisherman says about fishes is more likely to be true than the statements about fishes made by an army general who never goes fishing. But when it comes to military tactics, what the army general says is more likely to be true than the statements of the fisherman who has no military qualifications. Of course in saying that we are not saying that the fisherman never says anything wrong about fishes and fishing. He may, and sometimes he does. But that fact does not nullify the fact that when it comes to fishes and fishing, the fisherman is a better authority than one who rarely deals with fishes.

Now if a human being can have authority on account of special qualifications, much more does Jesus Christ. That is really an understatement. For the fact is that the authority of Jesus Christ cannot be compared to that of any human being since Jesus is the Son of God. Jesus Christ is unique. Being the supreme and final revelation of God, Jesus Christ knows as only God knows. So we put the highest premium on Jesus' view of Scripture.

When Jesus was here on earth, the New Testament books were not yet in existence—of course. So we are here concerned with what Jesus thought of the Bible that was then in existence, namely, the Old Testament.

There are many passages in the "Bible that indicate Jesus' attitude toward the Bible. Let us examine some of them.

There are people today who do not believe that Jonah was an actual person. They think the story of Jonah is too fantastic to be true. What did Jesus think of the Jonah story in the Old Testament? At Matthew chapter 12 we read that some of the scribes and Pharisees one day asked Jesus that he show them a sign. In reply, he told them that "an evil and adulterous generation" asks for a sign but that no sign would be given to such a generation "except the sign of the prophet Jonah." Then Jesus went on to tell them that Jonah was "three days and three nights in the belly of the whale." He told them that like Jonah the Son of man (i.e., Jesus) would be three days and three nights "in the heart of the earth." The men of Nineveh, he said, will condemn "this generation," for the Ninevites repented when they heard the preaching of Jonah. A greater than Jonah had come, Jesus said, referring to himself.

What shall we make of that? To me this indicates rather definitely that Jesus did believe in the historicity of Jonah; Jesus believed that the Jonah story is true. In clearly implying that the Jonah story in the Old Testament is true, Jesus affirmed the authority of Scripture.

Again, today there are people who do not believe in the story of Noah and the Great Flood. They put forth all kinds of arguments to the effect that there could not have been such a flood. What did Jesus think of the Noah story? One day Jesus was teaching his disciples. Part of what he said to them is recorded at Matthew 24:36-39. Concerning "the end of the age" Jesus told his disciples that no one, not even the angels of heaven, nor the Son, knew the day and hour; only the Father knows that, he said. Then he likened the coming of the Son of man to the days of Noah. As in Noah's time, before the flood people were eating and drinking and getting married, until the day when Noah entered the ark; they did not know until the flood came and swept them away. So will the return of the Son of man be, said he. Again, here we find Jesus affirming the Old Testament. He talked as a man who believed that Noah was an actual man, that there actually was a great flood, that people were actually drowned in the flood.

When Jesus was tempted by the devil, his reply to the devil was always preceded by 'It is written.' Thus he appealed to Scripture as authority.

Jesus criticized the Jews for searching the Scriptures and yet not knowing that the Scriptures testify of him; he chided them for not believing in him. (Luke 5)

Jesus affirmed the law and the prophets. He said that it is easier for heaven and earth to pass away than for a dot of the law to be invalidated. (Luke 16) He also said that he did not come to abolish the law and the prophets; he came to fulfill them. (Matthew 5)

At Matthew 19 we read that Jesus told some Pharisees who had come to test him that it was God who gave the law about marriage; so those who are joined together (in marriage) should not be "put asunder" by men.

After he had risen from the dead, Jesus told his disciples that everything written about him in the law of Moses, the prophets, and the psalms must be fulfilled. (Luke 24:44)

Let us examine some more passages. At Luke 16 we read

that Jesus told his disciples that the law and the prophets were "until John"; since then the good news of the kingdom had been preached. Jesus said it is easier for heaven and earth to pass away than for one dot of the law to be invalidated.

Another indication of Jesus' reliance on the authority of the Old Testament is his statement concerning what had been written about him "in the law of Moses and the prophets and the psalms." What had been written about him "must be fulfilled." (Luke 14:44) Here again we see a clear indication of Jesus' acceptance of the Old Testament. He believed the prophecies about him; he believed that what had happened in his career fulfilled those prophesies. What had been written in the Old testament spoke of Jesus' death and resurrection.

After his resurrection, Jesus continued to teach from the Scriptures. We read in Luke that the followers of Jesus had difficulty believing that he had indeed risen from the dead. While they were discussing together about the empty tomb, Jesus himself drew near and went with them. Jesus chided them for their slowness in believing what the prophets had said concerning him. He told them it was necessary that the Christ suffer the things that had happened to him. Beginning with Moses and all the prophets, Jesus interpreted to the disciples the passages concerning him. (Luke 24)

There are many more passages that clearly indicate that Jesus accepted the authority of the old Testament. Because Jesus Christ accepted the Scriptures as authoritative, they are authoritative. As Martin Kahler puts it, "we do not believe in Christ because we believe in the Bible, but we believe in the Bible because we believe in Christ."[1] Since Christ is the Lord of the church, and since Christ accepted the authority of the Old Testament, the church accepts the authority of the Old Testament. Now the Scriptures were not made the Word of God by the fact that Jesus recognized them to be from God; they were already from God before Jesus recognized them to be from God. As we have said earlier, the order of reality is logically prior to the order of knowledge. In point of time, the canon of the Old Testament had already been there before Jesus was born. The Jews had already recognized the Old

Testament writings to be from God. The significance of Jesus' recognition of the Old Testament as the Word of God is that we take the word of Jesus as true because of who Jesus is. We take the Old Testament as authoritative because Jesus took it as such.

Dr. A. Berkeley Mickelsen, Professor of New Testament Interpretation, lists verses in which the Old Testament writers clearly indicate that they were communicating God's word, not their own.[2] "There are four basic words or phrases in Hebrew that frequently declare that God has something to say in the pages of the Old Testament." Under each of the four expressions Mickelsen lists many passages in which the expression is used. The first expression means "utterance or declaration of Jehovah." "In every case the context stresses that the declaration is made by the covenant God of Israel. He is the Lord, Jehovah of Hosts."

The second expression, says Michelsen is the Hebrew verb translated "to speak." Here God asserts His authority. "In context these formulae introduce solemn utterances on the part of God to his people. The formulae occur over and over."

The third expression is the Hebrew verb "davar," which indicated that "God speaks and testifies to the authority of his own assertions."

The fourth expression indicating the authority of the Old Testament, is the noun "davar," "whose basic meaning is "speech" or "word." "this noun," says Mickelsen, "is employed extensively throughout the Old Testament."

The Old Testament prophets were spokesmen of God. Over and over again they prefaced what they said with "Thus says the Lord" (or some equivalent expression), thereby declaring that their message came from God, Not from themselves.

At I Samuel 15 we read that the prophet Samuel, whom God had earlier directed to anoint Saul king of the Israelites, told King Saul that God was directing him (Saul) to destroy the Amalekites, who had opposed the Israelites when they came from Egypt. When King Saul disobeyed the command of God by not killing all the animals, God again sent Samuel to King

Saul, this time to tell the king that God had rejected him as king because he had disobeyed God's order to destroy the Amalekites, including women, infants and animals. Samuel spoke with such authority to no less than the king of Israel; he had authority because he was God's messenger to the king. It was not his but God's authority he carried. In all his exchanges with King Saul, Samuel always made it clear to Saul that he was only delivering God's message. Saul always acknowledged that fact.

One prophet after another, the story is the same: the prophets were no more than messengers of God. And so it is that the entire Old Testament is God's word. The prophets were ordinary men; by themselves they had no authority. For example, Amos was a shepherd. But Amos spoke with great authority because he was sent by God to deliver God's word.

As for the authors of the New Testament books, again and again they claim they were writing as witnesses of the things they wrote about. The writer of the fourth Gospel explicitly states that his testimony is true because he himself was an eyewitness of the things he wrote about. (John 19:35)

Luke opens his Gospel with a statement concerning the reliability of the research he had done into the career of Jesus. In his prefatory statement, Luke acknowledged that many had undertaken to compile a narrative of the things that had happened and which had been delivered to them by eyewitnesses and ministers of the word. Luke told Theophilus, the one he was addressing in his prefatory remarks, that he himself had "followed all things closely for some time past" in order to be able to write his own orderly account. (Luke 1:1-4)

The rulers of the Jews did not like the fact that the followers of Jesus continued proclaiming Jesus crucified and risen from the dead. One day Peter and John were summoned by the Jewish leaders; they were told to stop speaking or teaching about Jesus. But Peter and John said that they could not but go on speaking of what they had seen and heard. They challenged the religious leaders to decide whether it was right in the sight of God to listen to them rather than God. (Acts 4)

The apostle Paul wrote many of the books of the New

Testament. He was not one of the early disciples of Jesus; in fact he was a zealous persecutor of Christians. But one day, when he was on the way to Damascus to persecute Christians, Christ appeared to him in a very dramatic way. Saul (his name was changed to Paul later) saw a light and heard a voice; the voice said he was Jesus whom he (Saul) was persecuting. That incident dramatically led to Saul's conversion. From that point on Saul was a very zealous proclaimer of the message of Christ; he suffered much in so doing because of the antagonism of the Jews, but he persevered. He too met Christ and he could not help telling Jews and Gentiles about his Lord. Paul knew whereof he spoke and wrote.

The Bible testifies to its own authoritativeness. II Timothy 3:16 states the matter pointedly: "All scripture is inspired by God and profitable for teaching, for reproof, for correction, and for training in righteousness." When this was written the Old Testament had been in existence; so this statement of Paul covers both the Old and the New Testaments. All scripture is inspired by God and therefore authoritative. At II Peter 2:20-21 we read: "First of all you must understand this, that no prophecy of scripture is a matter of one's own interpretation, because no prophecy ever came by the impulse of man, but men moved by the Holy Spirit spoke from God." This is such a clear statement that there is hardly any question as to what it is saying. The men who wrote what is now the Bible were "moved by the Holy Spirit"; they were guided by the Holy Spirit. They were not writing their own messages; they were communicating the word of God. Therefore what they wrote was authoritative; it was authoritative because it came from God.

There are many other passages we can cite to show how the Bible testifies to its being the word of God, to the truth of what it says. What we have cited is enough.

Now these affirmations are for Christians axiomatic. When a logician constructs a logical system he starts with one or more axioms, foundational propositions on which the entire logical system is built. All other propositions in the system (the theorems) are derived from the axioms by the use of the postulates of the system. In a sense we can think of the entire axiomatic system as an unfolding of the axioms. Since axioms are the starting, the foundational, propositions of the logical system, it makes no sense to demand that the logician prove the axioms. Theorems are proved—but not the axioms. The axioms are used in deriving theorems. If asked to justify his choice of axioms the logician constructing the system may respond by saying that he had no particular reasons. Choice is itself axiomatic; strictly speaking, one does not have to justify a choice. Of course one may if he chooses to, but it is legitimate to exercise a choice without offering any justifying considerations. Proving, justifying, logically must start somewhere; the alternative is an infinite regress. Let us now take a step backward and look at what we have done. We have argued that since Jesus Christ took the Old Testament writings as authoritative then they are authoritative. We have also quoted passages that state that the Bible is the word of God.

Now in objection, the unbeliever might say: "The trouble with quoting what Jesus said about the Old Testament and with quoting Bible passages to show that the Bible is the word of God is that that assumes the truth or the trustworthiness of the Bible documents. That's begging the question. The question precisely is whether what the Bible says is true, whether the Bible documents are reliable. You Christians quote from the Bible to support your belief that the Bible is authoritative. That's bad logic. Suppose that what is written in the Bible is not true, suppose that the Bible documents are not trustworthy. Then the supposed statements of Jesus Christ about the Bible cannot be accepted. In fact, the whole story of the life, ministry, death, and resurrection of Jesus of Nazareth cannot be accepted; the historicity of Jesus is suspect if not entirely false. And the Bible passages that state that the Bible is God's word turn out to be unacceptable if not entirely false. So we are back in square zero."

Before we reply, let us acknowledge that our reliance on Jesus' acceptance of the authority of the Old Testament is held in question if the New Testament documents are not trustworthy since the New Testament is our source of the story of Jesus.

If the New Testament documents that tell us about what Jesus said and did are not trustworthy, then our reliance on Jesus' endorsement of the authority of the Old Testament loses all its force. Our quoting Bible passages that state that the Bible is the word of God loses its evidentiary value if we cannot present any form of vindication of the Bible documents. If we cannot present any argument or evidence to support our belief in the Bible documents, then all our quoting from Jesus and from the Bible fails to establish our case.

So now let us exhibit the reasonableness of our position. Our preliminary reply to the unbeliever's objection is to point out that from the fact that the story of Jesus is in the Bible and the fact that the passages that say that the Bible is the word of God are in the Bible, it does not follow that the Bible is not the word of God or that what the Bible says is not true. This point may sound minor; but it is important and deserves being stated.

EXTERNAL EVIDENCE

A Parallel: A Bit of Logic

Another reply appeals to a phenomenon well-known outside the Bible. Of certain principles enunciated in the constitution of the United States it is affirmed, "We hold these truths to be self-evident." The American people have upheld the self-evidence of these principles for more than two hundred years now. And there are no indications that they will abandon these principles. The countries which are members of the United Nations have affirmed the United Nations Declaration of Human Rights. This Declaration affirms the self-evidence of a number of principles. Because these principles are taken as self-evident, they serve as fundamental principles to which the member countries of the United Nations have committed themselves. These principles are held in very high regard without the benefit of justification or vindication.

What is it about these principles which are declared as

self-evident and which the United States or the United Nations have adopted as fundamental principles? On the face of them, these self-evident principles appeal to these people as right and fundamental. For example, it is affirmed that human beings have certain inalienable rights simply because they are human beings. No human being may be denied these basic inalienable rights for reasons of nationality or education or skin color or age or economic status or whatever. There is something fundamentally right about that idea as far as the American people and the signers of the Declaration of Human Rights are concerned.

Of course there are people who actually disregard these principles that the United States and United Nations consider fundamental and right. There have been leaders of nations (for example, Hitler) who in practice have not valued these principles. But this fact does not make the principles any less right or any less fundamental as far as those who believe in them are concerned. The rightness and the "fundamentality" of these principles are not derived from their being recognized to be such. They are self-evident; they "carry in themselves" the quality of being right and fundamental. As we have said earlier, the order of reality must be distinguished from the order of knowing, the former being logically prior to the latter.

Now how is this reference to self-evident principles related to our discussion of the authority of the Bible? The analogical connection is as follows. There is nothing illogical or illegitimate about taking a set of principles as self-evidently right and fundamental or about taking a document as authoritative without the benefit of argument. There is nothing inherently illogical or illegitimate in taking a set of documents such as the Bible as one's starting point, as the foundation of one's system. If we examine systems of thought, we will find that each has certain fundamental ideas that serve as foundation. The authority of the Bible functions for Christians axiomatically. Just as the logician constructing a logical system must start with one or more foundational propositions, so does the Christian start with the authority of Scripture. And just as it is quite legitimate and proper for the logician constructing a logical system to choose any proposition(s) as his foundational propositions, so it is legitimate and proper for Christians to choose the Bible as the foundation of the Christian thought system. The Christian does not have to feel apologetic about the fact that he starts with the Bible, that he makes the Bible his ultimate appeal, his final authority. In general, we can say that whoever does any kind of thinking starts somewhere, and that somewhere is propositions. All reasoning, all proving, presupposes starting propositions. The demand that the believer in a system—any system— prove each and every item of his beliefs is a logically impossible, hence an unreasonable, demand.

Having accepted the Bible as his starting point, the Christian argues from the Bible in support of his beliefs and practice. There is nothing illogical or disrespectable in doing that.

Lest we be misunderstood it must be pointed out that while there is an analogical element between self-evident principles and the Bible, there is a serious disanalogy. In the case of self-evident principles, the appeal is only to the principles themselves; the reason for calling them self-evident is precisely that the principles are their own evidence; they are accepted as right or fundamental simply "on their own merit." Now in the case of the Bible, the Bible books are not accepted "on their own merit"; they are accepted as authoritative because they were written by men under the guidance and direction of the Spirit of God. The analogical point we are pointing out pertains only to their being accepted by adherents as starting points.

Now although Christians take the Bible as authoritative, as the foundation of their system, the Bible's authority is not ultimate. The ultimate authority is God. We have earlier quoted the passage that states that the men who wrote the Bible books were moved by the Holy Spirit; they spoke from God; they were giving God's message, not their own. (II Peter 1:20-21)

An analogy might help us here. (But as we offer this analogy let us be warned that in reasoning analogically it often happens that some elements in the objects analogized do not match; in the analogy I am offering here I mean to make use of only those points that I do mention in the analogy.) Let us take the case of the forming of the American Consitiution. A Constitutional Convention met. The members of the Convention were delegates, representatives of the people. And they were thinking and deliberating as the people's representatives. When the Constitution draft was finished it was submitted to the people for ratification. When it was approved by the people, it became the fundamental law of the land. Now the American Constitution has been amended more than once; changes have been made. Every change has to be ratified by the people. There is nothing to prevent the American people from totally discarding the present Constitution and constituting another one—should that be the desire of the majority of the people. Now here we see that the ultimate authority lies in the people, not in the constitution, neither in the delegates to the Constitutional Convention.

One analogical point has to do with the ultimacy of appeal. Cases brought before the courts are decided on the basis of statutes and of the Constitution. Questions of the constitutionality of certain laws are decided by the US Supreme Court on the basis of the Constitution. The final court of appeal is the Supreme Court; the final document to which the Supreme Court appeals is the Constitution. Now in a similar manner, Christians appeal to the Bible as their final authority. Questions of doctrine and action are decided on the basis of the Bible.

But there are disanalogies between the US Constitution and the Bible. One important disanalogy has to do with the ultimate source of authority. In the case of the Constitution, authority ultimately resides in the American people. That is why the people can, if they so desire, change part or all of the Constitution. On the contrary, the ultimate source of Biblical authority is God. This is a very big difference indeed.

Another important disanalogy is that whereas the Constitution may be changed in whole or in part—if the people so desire—it does not make sense to speak of the Bible being changed in whole or even in part. Being the written word of God, the Bible is final, once and for all time. Within the context of the Biblical system, it does not make sense to speak of God <u>revising</u> the revelation that now stands recorded in the Bible.

Some might in objection point out that there have been different versions of the Bible: the King James version, the Revised Standard version, the New International version, and so on. "Aren't these changes of the Bible?" No, these different translations are not changes of the Bible. After all, most of the translations go directly to the best available original language texts of the Bible. "Best" because the Bible scholars are always on the search for Bible documents that are older, more reliable, closer to the original. For example, in its Preface, the New International Version says: "The New International Version is a completely new translation of the Holy Bible made by over a hundred scholars working directly from the best available Hebrew, Armaic and Greek texts. It had its beginning in 1965 when. . . a group of scholars met . . . and concurred in the need for a new translation of the Bible in contemporary English." (Emphasis mine) As scholarship continues its work, new translations can be expected from time to time. The primary reason for making a translation of the Bible is to reflect the new findings of researchers. Archaeologists, Biblical critics, and other Bible scholars are always on the search for the more reliable Bible documents. Every small progress on the scholarship front is welcome news. As we will see later on in this chapter, the discoveries of archaeologists have helped a great deal in the scholars' effort to get closer to the original Bible documents. As new findings are accepted by the scholarly community, new translations are felt necessary.

Admittedly, not all translations are motivated by scholarly considerations. There are translations which are motivated primarily by the desire to make the Bible more readable by putting it in everyday English or in the vernacular. <u>Good News for Modern Man</u> is one such translation. In general, scholars would advise using the translations made <u>directly</u>

from the best available original language texts.

The point we are making here is that no matter how many translations of the Bible there may be, it is one and the same Bible that is being translated. There has always been and there will always be one and only one Bible.

We must respond further to the unbeliever's criticism of the Christian's reasoning from the Bible. Come to think of it, it is not just the Christian who reasons from something he accepts as a starting point. The fact is that in the twentieth century most if not all of the educated unbelievers are unbelievers because they start with the methods and criteria of science. The most dramatic evidence of this is the case of logical empiricism. In the first four decades of this century the philosophical movement called logical positivism (also known as logical empiricism) swept very much of the English-speaking world. So many philosophers in many countries became totally sold to the position of logical positivism. So many students became converts of it. But at the same time there were many who were dead earnest against logical positivism. Many philosophers were critical of it; all theologians were against it. Logical positivism was hotly debated for several decades. The intense debate started dying down in the 1940s.

Now what was it that made logical positivism so controversial? What was it that "enabled" it to dismiss as nonsense all of theology and all of traditional metaphysics? It was one idea—just one idea. The name of it was the Verifiability Principle. What is the Verifiability Principle? One problem in answering this question is that in the course of the long and bitter debate logical empiricists kept modifying their embattled criterion of meaningfulness. We will not go into the different formulations. It is enough to quote here just one formulation, that of Alfred Ayer, as stated in the Introduction to the second edition of his Language, Truth and Logic. Writes Ayer: "And I can now reformulate the principle of verification as requiring of a literally meaningful statement, which is not analytic, that it should be either directly or indirectly verifiable, in the foregoing sense" (p. 13). The verification spoken of is verification in terms of observation sentences. It was the empiricist aspect of the logical positivist movement that generated the heated controversy. Any word or sentence which did not point to anything that could be observed was counted as meaningless.

There you are. Just one idea gave the logical empiricists the weapon to throw out so much.

As can be expected, the bitter and long controversy in the end turned on the nature, the status, of the Verifiability Principle itself. Many argued that if the verification principle was applied to itself, it would render it meaningless, since it could not be verified by observation, neither was it an analytic statement. In the debate some tried to repair the embattled principle saying that it was a rule, not a statement, in which case it was not proper to apply it to itself. In the decades following the 1950s more and more philosophers abandoned the logical empiricist stance. Its extreme exclusiveness turned off many philosophers. Today logical empiricism is for all practical purposes dead. Other schools of thought in philosophy became popular: analytic philosophy, linguistic analysis, ordinary language philosophy.

But the spirit of logical empiricism is far from dead. Empiricism, which saw its initial blossoming in the early 18th century with the radical empiricism of David Hume (died 1776), remains very alive indeed in the1980s.The empiricist criterion of meaning and knowledge is still today very much   the starting point of many educated unbelievers . The tremendous advances of science and technology in our time enhance the adherence of many people to the empiricist criterion. For many it is their starting point. That is why they must dismiss revelation. And the "must" here is logical. If you adhere to the empiricist criterion of meaning and knowledge, then as a matter of logic you cannot believe in the supernatural since the logic of the supernatural is such that it cannot be known by means of empiricist techniques, or (which is really the same thing) the techniques of science. The empiricist has to look for all kinds of ways to explainaway that which to the Christian is the starting point, namely: revelation, the authority of Scripture. Today's educated unbeliever will give you all kinds of theories to account for the fact that so many millions of people in our day believe in God and in the Bible. And if you look carefully for the starting point of those theories, you will find that the empiricist criterion of meaning and knowledge lies at the bottom.

So who starts with something unargued? Is it only the Christian? It is, sir, also the unbeliever. If all the parties to the debate are logical and honest, before long it becomes clear that each starts from something unargued. The Christian starts with the Scriptures, with revelation: the unbeliever of today starts with the empiricist criterion of meaning and knowledge. Ultimately the ones listening in have to choose between the competing starting points. And that choice cannot be made on the basis of logic or argument, since the rules of inference are able to function only when at least one proposition is granted as a starting point. When the debate turns on the starting points of the opposing parties, logic is helpless. In the end, one has to choose between the ideas that the opposing parties start from without the help of the rules of logic. The Christian's reply to all parties is: As for me, I start with revelation, with the inspired Word of God. It is God's power for salvation to any one who has faith (Romans 1:16).

But that is not to say that that starting point is devoid of justification. As the following pages will show, there are considerations external to the Bible that converge to vindicate the Christian's adherence to the written word of God.

Early Testimony

Are the Gospels reliable? The earliest external evidence of the reliability of the Gospels comes from Papias, bishop of Hierapolis, who lived in the first half of the second century A.D. This statement is preserved in Eusebius' Ecclesiastical History III.39.[3]

And John the Presbyter also said this, Mark being the interpreter of Peter, whatsoever he recorded he wrote

with great accuracy, but not however, in the order in
which it was spoken or done by our Lord, for he
neither heard nor followed our Lord, but as before
said, he was in company with Peter, who gave him such
instruction as was necessary, but not to give a
history of our Lord's discourses: wherefore Mark
has not erred in any thing, by writing some things as
he has recorded them; for he was carefully attentive
to one thing, not to pass by any thing that he heard,
or to state any thing falsely in these accounts.

Such is the account written by Papias, as quoted by
Eusebius. Papias was bishop of Hierapolis in the first half of
the second century. If we trust Papias' account of Mark's
effort at being accurate in writing his Gospel, then we here
have an early external evidence of the reliability of the Gospel
of Mark. The unbeliever might question the accuracy of
Papias' report. But what reason would there be for Papias to
write a false account? What would be his motives? In the
absence of any clear evidence of motives that would lead the
bishop of Hierapolis to write a false account, we prefer to trust
Papias' account.

In the same chapter, Eusebius states that concerning
Matthew Papias wrote: 'Matthew composed his history in the
Hebrew dialect, and every one translated it as he was able.'

The Dates of the New Testament Writings

The dates of the New Testament writings can provide a
strong argument for the reliability of the Bible.

In the middle of the 19th century, the group of European
scholars known as the Tubingen school (from the name of the
University of Tubingen, where the leader of the group was a
professor), asserted that some of the most important books of
the New Testament, including the Gospels and Acts, did not
exist before the thirties of the second century A. D. "This
conclusion," according to F. F. Bruce, "was the result not of
any historical evidence but of philosophical presuppositions.

Even then there was sufficient historical evidence to show how unfounded these theories were . . . ' but the amount of such evidence available in our own day is so much greater and more conclusive that a first-century date for most of the New Testament writings cannot reasonably be denied, no matter what our philosophical presuppositions may be." (Bruce remarks that is a curious fact that historians have been much more ready than some theologians to trust the New Testament records. In a footnote Bruce says that historians like Ramsey, Meyer, and A. T. Olmstead "have protested vigorously against excessive skepticism of some theologians in dealing with the historical writings of the New Testament."[4] My own checking on this point confirms this remark of Bruce. One day I went to the main library of a major university in order to see if history books written by secular historians mention the events and persons of the Biblical documents. I consulted a number of books on ancient history. Every single one of them had chapters dealing with Old Testament and New Testament events and personalities. With the exception of one, the history books I consulted did not say anything that would hint that they did not consider the accounts reliable.)

Scholars differ as to exact dates of the writing of the New Testament books. In many cases the differences are slight. In the dates we are giving here we follow F. F. Bruce, who is highly respected among evangelical scholars. Bruce discusses the dates in Chapter II of his 1954 book, Are the New Testament Books Reliable?.

The New Testament was substantially complete around A.D. 100. According to Bruce, the majority of English scholars place the Gospel of Mark at c. 65, the Gospel of Luke at c. 80-85, the Gospel of Matthew, c. 85-90, the Gospel of John c. 90-100. Harnack and others, says Bruce, have given good reasons for assigning earlier dates to the first three Gospels: Mark and Luke, c. 60-65; Matthew, c. 70. Bruce says there are arguments for dating Acts around A.D. 60-62. Bruce dates the letters of Paul as follows: Galatians, A. D. 48; I and II Thessalonians, 50; Philippians, 54; I and II Corinthians, 54-56; Romans, 57; Colossians, Philemon, and Ephesians, c. 60;

the pastoral epistles, c. 63-64. Now it is generally held that Jesus Christ was crucified in A.D. 30.

The point that we want to make by mentioning these dates of the New Testament books is that they were written <u>shortly after</u> the events they were about.. When the books were written there were still people living who saw and heard the events narrated by the New Testament writing. When we consider how momentous the events were, especially the crucifixion and resurrection of Jesus, it is not difficult to believe that the people still living when the New Testament books were written still clearly remembered what happened. It is probable that many of those who were healed miraculously by Jesus or the disciples and many of those who were eyewitnesses to the miracles were still living when some of the New Testament books were written. Had there been false statements made by the New Testament writers, such could have been exposed by the eyewitnesses of the events who were still living.

The Bible Versus Other Ancient Writings

It strikes me as quite interesting that when it comes to the Bible documents many people raise questions pertaining to the trustworthiness of the documents. There seems to be so much fuss about the reliability of the Biblical documents. And yet when it comes to secular ancient documents, such as the writings of Homer, Euripides, the pre-Socratic philosophers, Plato, Aristotle and many other ancients acceptance of the documents as they have come down to us is so much easier. And yet many of the secular ancient writings that are accepted without fuss are old. For example, Homer flourished in the 9th century B.C., Aeschylus in the 6th century B.C., Euripides in the 5th century B.C., Thucydides in the 5th century B.C., Plato in the 5th century B.C., Aristotle in the 4th century B.C.. But students reading the works of these classic authors do not raise the question of the reliability of the texts that have come down to us. Students writing papers on issues in Plato engage in meticulous analysis of the English translation of Plato without asking if the Greek texts of Plato are reliable. In all the philosophy courses I took as a student, even in graduate school, I did not hear a single student—or professor—raise the question of whether the text of the pre-Socratics or Plato or Aristotle or some other ancient philosopher was reliable. If any of my classmates or professors had any doubts about the trustworthiness of the ancient writings we were studying they kept those doubts to themselves; I never heard any. Students read the classics believing that the texts are trustworthy. But when it comes to the Bible documents, there seems to be so much resistance. Is it because of the unwillingness of people to accept revelation? Is it because the Bible's authority rests on God?

I am not saying this because we Christians do not want such inquiry—we do. I am saying it only because the disparity in treatment of the documents needs to be noticed. We do welcome the question. It is important to address the question of the trustworthiness of the Biblical documents as documents. Such an inquiry gives the Christian the opportunity to show the evidence upon which the Christian's trust in the Biblical documents rests.

So let us now focus our attention on the question: Are the Bible documents as documents reliable? Are they trustworthy? How do they compare with other ancient writings with respect to reliability?

In the preface of his 1954 book Are the New Testament Documents Reliable ? F. F. Bruce, Professor of Biblical Criticism and Exegesis at the University of Manchester, a scholar highly regarded among evangelical scholars, writes:[5]

I have written as one who was for nineteen years a
student and teacher of classics in various
Universities, with the purpose of showing that the
grounds for accepting the New Testament as reliable
compare very favorably with those on which the
classical student accepts the authenticity and
credibility of many ancient documents. It is not
usually possible to demonstrate by historical

arguments the truth of every detail in an ancient writing, whether inside or outside the Bible. It is sufficient to have reasonable confidence in a writer's general trustworthiness; if that is established, there is an <u>a priori</u> likelihood that his details are true. In historical research, as in many other things, probability, in Bishop Butler's words, 'is the very guide to life.'

On pp. 19-23 of this book, Bruce lines up data that give to the books of the New Testament a very strong edge over other ancient documents.[6]

The evidence for our New Testament writings is ever so much greater than the evidence for many writings of classical authors, the authenticity of which no one dreams of questioning. And if theNew Testament were a collection of secular writings, their authenticity would generally be regarded as beyond doubt. . . .

There are in existence about 4,000 Greek manuscripts of the New Testament in whole or in part. The best and most important of these go back to somewhere about A.D. 350, the two most important being the Codex Vaticanus, the chief treasure of the Vatican Library in Rome, and well-known Codex Sinaiticus, which the British Government purchased from the Soviet Government for 100,000 [British pounds] . . . and which is now the chief treasure of the British Museum. Two other important early MSS in this country [Great Britain] are the Codex Alexandrinus, also in the British Museum, written in the fifth century, and the Codex Bezae, in Cambridge University Library, written in the fifth or sixth century, and containing the Gospels and Acts in both Greek and Latin.

Perhaps we can appreciate how wealthy the New Testament is in manuscript attestation if we compare the textual material for other ancient historical works. For Caesar's Gallic War (composed between 58 and 50 B.C.) there are several extant MSS, but only nine or ten are good, and the oldest is some 900 years later than Caesar's day. Of the 142 books of the Roman History of Livy (19 B.C.-A.D. 17) only 35 survive; these are known to us from not more than twenty MSS of any consequence . . . . Of the fourteen books of the Histories of Tacitus (c. A.D. 100) only four and a half survive; of the sixteen books of his Annals, ten in full and two in part. . . . .The History of Thucydides (c. 460-400 B.C.) is known to us from eight MSS, the earliest belonging to c. A.D. 900, and a few papyrus scraps, belonging to about the beginning of the Christian era. The same is true of the History of Herodotus (c. 480-425 B.C.). Yet no classical scholars would listen to an argument that the authenticity of Herodotus or Thycydides is in doubt because the earliest MSS of their works which are of any use to us are over 1,300 years later than the originals.

But how different is the situation of New Testament in this respect! In addition to the two excellent MSS of the fourth century, the earliest of some thousands known to us, considerable fragments remain of papyrus copies of books of the New Testament dated from 100 to 200 years earlier still..... A more recent discovery consists of some papyrus fragments dated by papyrological experts not later than A.D. 150 . . . .

Earlier still is a fragment of a papyrus codex containing John xviii. 31-33, d7f., now in the John Rylands Library, Manchester, dated by Deissmann and others in the reign of Hadrian (A.D. 117-138), showing that the latest of the four Gospels, which was written, according to tradition, at Ephesus between A.D. 90 and 100, was circulating in Egypt within about forty years of its composition . . . . This must be regarded as the earliest fragment, by at least fifty years, of the New Testament.

Attestation of another kind is provided by allusions to and quotations from the New Testament books in other early writings. The authors known as the Apostolic Fathers wrote chiefly between A.D. 90 and 160, and in their works we find evidence for their acquaintance with most of the books of the New Testament.

Sir Frederick G. Kenyon, formerly director and principal librarian of the British Museum, speaking of the New Testament documents, writes:[7]

In no other case is the interval of time between the composition of the book and the date of the earliest extant manuscripts so short as in that of the New Testament. The books of the New Testament were written in the latter part of the first century; the earliest extant manuscripts (trifling scraps excepted) are of the fourth century—say, from 250 to 300 years later. This may sound a considerable interval, but it is nothing to that which parts most of the great classical authors from their earliest manuscripts. We believe that we have in all essentials an accurate text of the seven extant plays of Sophocles; yet the earliest substantial manuscript upon which it is based was written more 1400 years after the poet's death. Aeschylus, Aristophanes, and Thucydides are in the same state; while with Euripides the interval is increased to 1600 years. For Plato it may be put at 1300 years, for Demosthenes as low as 1200.

Those words were written by Kenyon in 1912. In the following years archaeologists discovered numerous papyri portions of the New Testament documents. These papyri portions go back to as early as the end of the first century, thus bridging the 250 to 300 years gap [8]   Commenting on the findings of archaeology, in 1940 Kenyon wrote in his book The Bible and Archaeology:[9]

> The interval, then, between the dates of original composition and the earliest extant evidence becomes so small as to be in fact negligible, and the last foundation for any doubt that the Scriptures have come down to us substantially as they were written has now been removed. Both the Authenticity and the general integrity of the books of the New Testament may be regarded as finally established. (Kenyon's emphasis)

Archaeological Evidence

Now let us focus on verification. Among the several theories of truth that philosophers have advanced since the days of the ancients, the most widely accepted is the correspondence theory. According to the correspondence theory of truth, a statement is true if what it says is so. And the way to determine the truth of a given statement is to check, to verify. If the statement says that five men died in the flood that swept Town A last week, we go and investigate; we ask the people in Town A; we ask the relatives of those who drowned; we ask the police; we ask one of the ministers in town A. We go to the cemetery of Town A. We inspect the place where the five were said to have drowned. We read the newspapers of Town A, the issues of the day of the drowning and the issues of the following day. If we find that the circumstances were as the statement says they were, then we say the statement is true.

It is easy to see why the correspondence theory of truth is the most widely accepted not only among philosophers but also among other people. It is a common sense conception of truth. Every courtroom trial of a criminal case emphasizes the correspondence theory of truth. The judge's goal is to determine what actually happened.

I am making this remark about the correspondence theory

of truth because now we are going to introduce in our defense of the trustworthiness of the Bible a new science, one that has tremendously boosted the reliability of the Bible documents as documents by the data it has unearthed. Many Bible statements that have been questioned or doubted or dismissed as outright false have been confirmed by the findings of archaeology. E. M. Blaiklock has called archaeology "one of the wonders of this century."[11] Archaeology is a science that has been making such great progress that definitions of the term "archaeology" formulated when the science was just starting are no longer adequate. After citing two earlier definitions as inadequate, Blaiklock offers the following definition (1984): "Archaeology is that branch of historical research that draws its evidence from surviving material traces and remains of past human presence and activity."[10]

The science of archaeology is only a little more than a century old, but it has already provided a very impressive amount of data about the past. Let us quote again from Blaiklock's 1984 book Archaeology of the NewTestament revised edition.[11]

Today the object of [archaeological] investigation are much more comprehensive and widespread. From the care with which the very chalk marks on a street wall of Pompeii are preserved to the minute accuracy with which fragments from a Qumran Cave are measured, marks the widening scope and the advancing method of the archaeologist. . . . From aerial Photography to Carbon 14 dating, the archaeologist has multiplied and improved his tools and methods, and these developments show no sign of abating. . The vast increase in historical knowledge thus achieved is one of the wonders of this century. . . . . before archaeological research began to make contributions to biblical studies, supplementary sources for the history contained in the Old and New Testaments were exceedingly scarce. But now, thanks to the probing spade, there exists a great body of texts and artifacts that greatly enrich our understanding of the Bible and the history teaching it contains. Indeed our knowledge of the Bible has been transformed.

In concluding his Archaeology and the Old Testament (1958), James Prichard says:[12]

... the archaeologist who went out to the lands of the Bible found far more than he had expected. At most, the span of time covered by the Bible is two thousand years; the mounds and caves of the Near East have borne evidence to document human culture extending over a period of several times the length of this biblical span. Jericho was a walled city some four thousand years or more before its walls fell before Joshua, and the cities of lower Mesopotamia had a written literature some fifteen hundred years before Abraham left Ur. . . . . Modern research has not only extended the time span of antiquity; it has enlarged the area of the known ancient world. New peoples, with languages which have been deciphered and translated, have made their appearance on the scene, In the rich harvest of written materials which have come from what was once called narrowly "Bible lands," new claims for detailed research have been staked out; special disciplines have arisen, such as Egyptology, Hititology, Sumerology, and Akkadian and Ugaritic studies. . . . .Peoples once known only from the Bible, for so many centuries the sole witness to the pre-Greek world, have now been recovered and documented from other sources. The map of ancient history has been filled in, to provide a better view of both a history of human culture and the distinctive contribution of the people of Israel. It is fair to claim, I think, that the Bible has moved . . . out of the isolation which it has for centuries enjoyed as "sacred" into the main stream of world history. (Emphasis added)

In the nineteenth century there were European scholars who held a negative view of the Gospel of Luke. Sir William Ramsay spent years of archaeological and geographical research on Luke. After his years of study he wrote, 'Luke's history is unsurpassed in respect of its trustworthiness.'[13]

In the case of ancient writings, both secular and religious, the one problem scholars face in their endeavor to get at what exactly the writer wrote is that the original writings are no longer available. In many cases of ancient writings, scholars have to work from fragments or quotations by later writers from what an earlier writer said. It is an occasion of great excitement when the scholar comes upon a document that is older and not so fragmentary. The more complete the copy, the more helpful it is. Classics scholars are always in the search for better manuscripts, for older manuscripts that will give them a better idea of the original.

In one sense the Biblical documents are in a better position than the secular ancient documents. In the case of the Bible documents, there are many scholars spending countless hours in meticulous study of documents and artifacts discovered by archaeological projects for Biblical research. Advanced technologies are employed in deciphering what the archaeologists bring to the surface in their excavations. What for? To better determine the wording of the original Biblical documents.

There is one thing about archaeological finds: they are data. You can interpret data but you cannot argue against them. When a scholar's theory conflicts with data discovered by archaeologists, the scientific attitude is to prefer the data.

What some have called revolutionary in the history of Biblical research is the discovery of scrolls hidden for centuries in caves in the Dead Sea area. It all began quite accidentally. Two Bedouin shepherds searching for a stray goat accidentally discovered a cave at Qumran, on the northwestern end of the Dead Sea. In the cave they found earthenware jars. One jar contained decaying bundles of leather scrolls. They sold the scrolls to an antique dealer in Bethlehem. It turned out that those scrolls were of great significance to Biblical research into the background of Christianity. That accidental discovery by shepherds led to excavations by archaeologist in the Dead Sea area. Some three hundred caves have been excavated and eleven of these caves contained written scrolls. The different types of manuscripts included Biblical writings and commentaries on Biblical books.[14]

As the experts study these documents meticulously, they see more and more how valuable the Dead Sea Scrolls are for Bible research. As William Brownlee puts it:[15]

> The most obvious value of the Qumran Scrolls [that's another name given to the Dead Sea Scrolls] is for determining the authentic text of the Old Testament, since indeed every book of the Hebrew Bible (unless it be Esther) is represented among the manuscript fragments of the fourth Qumran cave alone. Prior to the discovery of the Qumran Scrolls our direct knowledge of the Hebrew Old Testament text was limited largely to the text of the Rabbinic Judaism, which is known as the Massoretic [meaning, traditional] text. (Emphasis mine)

F. F. Bruce, who is considered one of the experts on the Dead Sea Scrolls, writes:[16]

> If it was indeed true, as the first scholars to examine the scrolls claimed, that they belonged to the early years A.D., or the closing centuries B.C., then we had Hebrew Biblical manuscripts nearly a thousand years nearer to the time at which the Old Testament books were written than the earliest that were previously known. (Emphasis added)

Bruce goes on to say that further evidence seems to confirm the early dating of the scrolls. In 1939, Bruce tells us, Sir Frederick Kenyon asked, 'Does this Hebrew text, which we call Massoretic, and which we have shown to descend from a text drawn up about A.D. 100, faithfully represent the Hebrew books?' Bruce says this 'great, indeed all important question' "is well on the way to receiving a much more explicit and positive answer than was thought possible then."[17]

Biblical scholars are still continuing their study of the Dead Sea Scrolls. As a result of the labors of archaeologists and Biblical textual scholars our confidence in the trustworthiness of the Bible documents is increasing.

The Canon

"We hold these truths to be self-evident, that all men are created equal, that etc." All men are created equal. What do you think of this principle? Most people would accept this principle. Many would say it is a very fundamental principle. The framers of the American Constitution and the United Nations Declaration of Human Rights consider the principle self-evident and fundamental. They accept it not on the basis of argument but simply because of itself. What the principle says appeals to them as right—without any presentation of evidence or argument. In other words, there is something about the principle—there is something in the principle—that makes it right and fundamental. Those who believe it to be a self-evident and fundamental principle would say that any-one who understands the principle would accept it.

The reason I am talking about the acceptance of a principle as self-evident is that a self-evident principle in one respect resembles Scripture. In the history of the Christian church two important processes were the constitution of the list of writings that is now the Old Testament and the constitution of the list of writings that is now the New Testament. We could speak of it as the formation of the canon—or, simpler, the compilation of the list of God-inspired books. The resemblance between the acceptance of self-evident principles and the formation of the canon is this: the leaders of the early Christian church accepted the books that now compose the Old and the New Testaments because they saw in the writings that they were written by God's inspiration. It was something about the writings that "told" the church leaders that they were inspired writings. The one criterion that made a writing qualify into the list (the canon) was that it was inspired—it was believed to be a God-inspired writing. If there was serious doubt as to whether it was inspired, it was not included in the canon.

The books that were accepted into the canon were by that fact accepted by the church as the standard, the rule of faith and practice. From the time that the canon was constituted to this day the Bible books have been taken as the rule of faith and practice. Questions of belief and conduct are decided against what is written in the books of the Bible as we now have them.

We must emphasize one thing here, namely: that the acceptance of a given writing into the list (the canon) was based on its authority, on its being seen as inspired by God. In other words, authority is logically and historically prior to canonicity—not the other way around. So canonicity is one external evidence of Biblical authority.

The unbeliever might say, "But what assurance do we have that the early church leaders were correct in believing that the books they admitted into the canon were inspired by God? How sure can we be that their judgment was sound?" Our answer is that Jesus told his followers that when the Holy Spirit came he (the Holy Spirit) would guide the church into all truth. Just as the men who wrote the books of the Bible wrote under the inspiration of the Holy Spirit, so the men who decided which writing were to be included in the canon did so under the guidance of the Holy Spirit. Now we do not expect the unbeliever to be able to make sense of this talk about the guidance of the Holy Spirit. But his inability to make any sense of this talk does not imply that this talk is nonsense or that it is not true. All it means is that the unbeliever is not able to understand what to the believer is a great truth. Argumentum ad ignorantiam (arguing from ignorance) is a fallacy.

Fulfilled Prophecies

Another external evidence of the authority of Scripture is fulfilled prophecies. Nowhere in all literature is there evidence of prediction made long before fulfilled. It is only in the Bible where we have many instances of the fulfillment of prophecies uttered many years earlier.

There being many instances of fulfilled prophecies recorded in the Bible, we will not look at all of them.

Chapter 53 of the book of Isaiah reads very much like it was written after the death of Jesus of Nazareth. The description in this chapter of Isaiah fits amazingly well the circumstances of Jesus' death. And yet the book of Isaiah was written in the eighth century B.C. How did Isaiah know that that was how Jesus was going to die? The hypothesis that it was all coincidence does not explain the amazing fact that the description in Isaiah 53 so nicely fits the actual circumstances of Jesus' death.

If the Isaiah description were alone, we might dismiss it as coincidence, although it would surely be a very unusual coincidence. But what is impressive is the number of fulfilled prophecies recorded in Scripture. In Luke 24 we read that after his resurrection, in one of Jesus' appearances before his disciples, Jesus reminded the disciples of the words he had spoken to them while he was still with them, that everything written about him in the law of Moses and the prophets and the psalms must be fulfilled. He told them that it had been written that the Christ would suffer and that he would rise from the dead on the third day, and that forgiveness of sins should be preached in his name to the whole world, beginning from Jerusalem. Here we have Jesus himself affirming that what had been written in the Old Testament about him had been fulfilled.

Again in Luke 24, after Jesus' resurrection, he appeared to two men walking to Emmaus. He asked them what they were talking about. The two men were surprised that the man who drew near and walked with them had not heard about the big events that had happened concerning Jesus of Nazareth. And they told him about the crucifixion of Jesus. They also told him about how some the other disciples went to the tomb of Jesus and found that it was empty. At that point in the conversation Jesus said to them that they were "slow of heart to believe" what the prophets had spoken. He told them that it was necessary that the Christ should suffer. Then Jesus instructed them in the Scriptures, showing them what had been written about him. When Jesus said this to the two men, they still did not know it was Jesus who had drawn near and walked with them. It was only later, at the breaking of the bread, that they recognized that the man was Jesus.

At Matthew 5:17-19 Jesus is quoted as saying that he had come not to abolish but to fulfill the law and the prophets. He said that not an iota would pass from the law until everything was accomplished. There is no need to lay out here all the many references to fulfilled prophecies. What we have cited is enough to make our point that fulfilled prophecies constitute one strong external evidence of the trustworthiness, the authority, of Scripture.

The Unity of the Bible

Another evidence of the trustworthiness of the Bible is its amazing unity. In secular literature, we find that those who have written about reality, principally the philosophers, have exhibited quite a bit of theoretical disunity. One who studies the history of philosophy, from its very beginnings to the present, will not fail to notice one thing: disagreement, endless disagreement. Even philosophers belonging to the same generation and living in the same country disagree on all kinds of things. The pre-Socratic philosophers talked about the nature of the world; they came up with differing ideas. Yes, there are what one might call schools of thought in philosophy, for example, logical positivism, but the position of one school is opposed by other schools of thought. Also, even within a given school of thought philosophers do not agree on everything; you find them criticizing each other's specific ideas. That's why the philosophy journals always have articles to publish.

With the Bible the situation is quite different. The writing of the Bible took place within fifteen centuries. The more than forty authors differed widely in educational, social, economic backgrounds. They lived in different environments.

They were of different ages. Now the amazing thing is that in spite of the factors that separated the writers from one another the sixty-six books of the Bible are united under one clear theme: the redemption of man. That thread runs through the whole Bible. The entire Bible centers on Jesus Christ. All the books of the Bible clearly exhibit the same one purpose. Prophecies uttered centuries earlier came about, as we have mentioned earlier. This amazing unity of the Bible is another evidence of its authority, of its having been written under the direction of guidance of the Holy Spirit. In this aspect of the Bible differs from all other collections of sacred writings. Roland K. Harrison, Professor of Old Testament, writes: [18]

> These ["the so-called 'Bibles' of the heathen religions] . . . have no unity. They are accumulations of heterogeneous materials, presenting in their collocation embody no historical revelation working out a purpose in consecutive stages from germinal beginnings to perfect close. The Bible, by contrast, is a single book because it embodies such a revelation and exhibits such a purpose. The unity of the book, made up of so many parts, is the attestation of the reality of the revelation it contains.

If someone is inclined to doubt what we have said about the Bible's unity, we can only invite him to read it. If he reads it from beginning to end with a mind truly open, he will himself see what millions of believers through these centuries have seen.

Experience as Evidence

Now we come to the evidence from Christian experience. Christian religious experience is another source of data supporting the authority of Scripture. But before we say anything more on this subject, a qualification must be stated. In saying that experience is one source of data for Biblical authority we do not mean to guarantee the veridicality of any and every report of Christian God-related experience. Christians' reports of God-related experiences can be exaggerated, inaccurate, or outright false. But at the same time, it must be stated that the fact that some reports of Christian God-related experience can be inaccurate or even false does not entail that no such reports are true. Each experience must be validated. In evaluating the report, we must take into account the character and reputation of the person making the report. We must consider his possible motives for making the report. A thorough inquiry would look into the reporter's mental and bodily state at the time of the reported experience. The circumstances obtaining at the time when the experience was supposed to have occurred should also be taken into account. Given all that caution, and admitting the possibility that a given report by a Christian of a God-related experience can be inaccurate or even false, still we maintain that God-related experiences do occur among Christians. And those experiences confirm the promises the Christian reads in the Bible, thus helping to establish Biblical authority.

Experience confirms the authority of Scripture in the following way. The person who already believes in the Bible takes seriously the promises of God he reads in the Bible. Now one of the forms of prayer is petition, in which the Christian brings certain concerns for himself or for others before God. It is usually in connection with petitionary prayer that the Christian comes to have experiences that confirm what is written in the Bible.

There are conditions stated in the Bible for answered prayer. One of the conditions is faith. The New Testament narrates situations in which a sick person was healed by Jesus and Jesus told the person, 'Your faith has made you well.'

Cases of answered prayer are not limited to Biblical persons. In the two thousand years of Christianity, there have been countless instances of God answering prayer. Most of the instances have not been published. Christians sometimes testify to answered prayer to friends in private or in Sunday school or in the larger church congregation.

But some instances of answered prayer have been published. One such book is George Mueller's Answers to Prayer, a very inspiring book. In this book Mueller simply narrates the situations in which he prayed and experienced God's answer. Mueller was an outstanding modern man of faith. He felt led by God to put up an orphanage in Bristol, England in the 19th century. But taking care of the needs of orphans was not Mueller's primary purpose in establishing the orphanage; it was of course a major purpose but it was not his primary purpose. His primary purpose was to demonstrate to the modern world by means of that project that God answers prayer. From the very start Mueller determined that he was not going to ask for money or goods from any human being for the needs of the orphanage. His fund-raising method was simply to pray. And that is exactly how he ran the orphanage to the very end of his long involvement in it. Not a single time did Mueller ask any human being for a cent or for a loaf of bread for the orphanage. He admitted hundreds of orphans into the orphanage. How were the needs of food, shelter, health care, recreation, and education of the orphans met? Simply by prayer. There are very moving instances narrated in this book. People sent money or goods without having been asked. For example, there were nights when there was not enough food for the next day's breakfast. Mueller asked God for food for the following morning. Before breakfast time the following day someone had brought food to the orphanage. There was never a day when the orphans did not have enough food. The accounts of answered prayer are so impressive and yet they are told very simply, as is usual with men of great faith. The glory is ascribed to God.

Now an unbeliever reading Mueller's book would very likely drop it as hogwash. "Who can believe that stuff?" would be the unbeliever's likely reaction. And that would not be at all surprising. Only one who believes in God, who believes that God answers prayer, can really understand Mueller's book. Only one who has experienced answered prayer can appreciate Mueller's accounts of specific prayers answered.

Experiences of God's working in one's life go a long way in strengthening one's belief in the Bible. In all these years since I began my studies in philosophy, I have read so many atheist and agnostic writings of philosophers. I have sat under atheist and agnostic professors. Two of my professors were particularly vocal in class about their atheism. But through it all my faith has grown. One reason is that my wife and I have had definite experiences of answered prayer. There is something about experience that withstands the arguments of unbelievers: you know it happened. You know the thing you asked of God; you know the specific circumstances of your praying. And you know what happened as a result of your prayer. But of course the whole interpretation is done in the context of faith. As the Bible puts it, without faith it is impossible to please God. Faith is a basic requisite for answered prayer. And that is the dividing line between those who believe that God answers prayer and those who cannot even make sense of this kind of talk. As the apostle Paul expresses it, the gifts of the Spirit of God are foolishness to the unspiritual man; he is unable to understand them because they are spiritually understood. (I Cor. 2:14)

In his book God and Philosophy the atheist philosopher Anthony Flew has a chapter devoted to attacking religious experience. In my reading of this chapter I got the impression that the big difference Flew and those who believe in the "validity" of God-related experience is that Flew has not had any kind of experience resembling the Christian's experience of God's working in his life. I got the impression that there really is no debate between Flew and his opponents; the two sides differ so very widely that there is no meeting on any issue. But the issues are important, and Flew realizes that fact. He insists that the disagreement between him and Christians on the subject of religious experience is far more than merely academic. In fact it is interesting that on this topic Flew seems at times to be irritated. Normally, Flew writes as a cool, analytical philosopher. But in this chapter there are places in which he loses his analytical coolness; his language turns harsh.

Now what does the unbeliever's lack of experience of answered prayer prove? What does his unbelief about God-related experience prove? Does it establish that there is no such thing as God answering a believer's prayer? Granted that there are many people who have never experienced answered prayer. Granted that there are many people who do not believe at all in God. What do those facts establish? Surely those facts cannot establish that there is no such thing as God-related experience. If something has happened, it has happened even if no single human being believes it did. Suppose that in the middle of the night there was a lot of thunder and lightning but that all the people in the town were sound asleep. No one heard the thunder or saw the lightning. Does that mean there was no thunder and no lightning?

The conversion of the apostle Paul is very instructive. Saul (his name was later changed to Paul) was a Pharisee, a religious leader in Israel. He was a highly educated man. Saul the Pharisee was an ardent enemy of the followers of Jesus Christ. He was zealous in persecuting Christians. In the Book of Acts, Chapter 9, we read the account of Paul's conversion. We read that the Pharisee Saul, filled with murderous anger toward the followers of Christ, went to the high priest and asked him for letters to the Damascus synagogues. He wanted to go to Damascus to look for believers in Christ, to take them to Jerusalem as prisoners. When he was nearing Damascus, he saw a light from heaven flash around him. He fell to the ground. He heard a voice calling to him, 'Saul, Saul, why do you persecute me?' Saul asked the owner of the voice who he was; and the reply was that he was Jesus. The owner of the voice told Saul to get up and enter Damascus; Saul would be told what to do. Those who were traveling with Saul heard the voice but saw no one; they were speechless. Saul stood up; he could not see anything. His companions led him by the hand into Damascus City. For three days Saul remained blind. For three days he neither ate nor drank.

In the city of Damascus there lived one Ananias, a disciple. In a vision Ananias was instructed by Christ to go to the street called Straight and to ask at the house of Judas about Saul of Tarsus. Ananias told the Lord that he had heard that this man Saul of Tarsus had done much evil to the followers of Christ; he said Saul was in Damascus with authority from the religious leaders in Jerusalem to round up believers in Christ. The Lord told Ananias to go and do what he was told to do. The Lord said he had chosen Saul as his instrument to proclaim God's name among the Gentiles and before kings and the sons of Israel. Ananias went. He laid his hands on Saul, telling Saul that Jesus had sent him so Saul could regain his sight and be filled with the Holy Spirit. Immediately Saul regained his sight. And then and there he was baptized.

Saul stayed with the disciples of Christ in Damascus. In the synagogues of the Jews he immediately proclaimed Jesus as the Son of God. People who heard him were quite surprised; they had heard about Saul's persecution of those who believed in Christ. But Saul confounded the Jews of Damascus by arguing that Jesus was indeed the Christ.

That is how Saul was converted to Christ. It happened rather quickly for a man of such education and such zeal in persecuting Christians. The experience on the road to Damascus did it all.

That Damascus Road experience was the turning point of Saul's life. After his conversion he immediately became a zealous follower of the Way. He preached to Jews and to non-Jews (=Gentiles). Paul was stoned, beaten, imprisoned; his life was constantly threatened. But he kept on preaching Christ to the very end of his life. Paul's story is one outstanding example of the influence of God-related experience. Those who would doubt the sincerity of Saul's conversion are reminded that the test of the genuineness of Saul's conversion was what happened in the following years. To the very end of his days Paul preached Christ under all kinds of danger and hardship.

God-related experiences go a long way in strengthening a believer's conviction concerning the authority of Scripture.

Having said what we have said in the preceding paragraphs, let us now entertain an unbeliever's objection. Let us examine an argument by Antony Flew, in the chapter we have earlier referred to. Flew believes that the subject of religious experience is important because he sees that it is used to support the belief in revelation. He asks, "Suppose it does seem to us that we are 'encountering God,' how can we tell whether or not we really are?" He calls this "our sixty-four-dollar question." This being most important point in his chapter on experience, let us quote him.[19]

> ... the question arises precisely because it is impossible to make direct and self-authenticating <u>inferences</u> from the character of the subjective experience to conclusions about the supposedly corresponding objective facts. <u>The impossibility here is logical</u>. It is not ... that it just so happens that as a matter of fact there are not in any subjective experience any distinguishing marks the presence of which <u>necessarily</u> guarantees that that particular experience must be veridical. It is rather that there <u>necessarily</u> could not be such marks, providing a guarantee which was itself <u>necessarily</u> reliable.

We have in quoting added emphasis to call attention to key phrases or words. Notice the sentence "The impossibility here is logical." This is the key sentence in this passage. What does this sentence signify? What is behind it? Why should we be dealing with a logical impossibility when we are talking about God and experience? God and experience are not matters of logic; they are matters of fact. God and experience belong in the domain of reality—not in the domain of logic. Notice also how many times the "necessarily" occurs. Now the word "necessarily" belongs in the domain of logic, not of matters of fact. Why should Flew keep using the word "necessarily" in this passage? Again that tells us that as far as Flew's thinking is concerned we are dealing with logical matters—not matters of fact. And right there is a place where we must object vehemently. When it is God and experiences we are talking about, we are dealing with matters of fact, not matters of logic.

Flew is saying that in any experience it is <u>logically</u><u>impossible</u> to conclude from the character of the experience to any corresponding objective facts; he is saying that from the character of any experience it is impossible to conclude to the existence of God to which the experience is supposed to be related. There is nothing in the nature of experience—any experience—that <u>necessarily</u> guarantees that the experience is indeed related to God.

In order to make clear the point we are trying to make against Flew, let us first distinguish between matters of fact and matters of logic, between logical impossibility and physical or practical impossibility. Given that A is less than B and B less than C, then it is logically impossible that C is less than A. The impossibility is due to the meaning of the expression "less than." We do not even know what A or B or C is; it is enough that we know their relationship to each other. The relationship is that A is less than B and B less than C. In logical impossibility we are concerned only with ideas—not with what is happening in the world, not with matters of fact.

Let us have another example. Given the <u>definition</u> of "circle" and the <u>definition</u> of "square," then if a certain figure is a square it is logically impossible for it to be a circle. The reason why a square cannot be a circle is that <u>by their definitions</u> one cannot be the other. The kind of impossibility is logical. The impossibility is not due to reality or matters of fact; it is due simply to the definitions involved. Definitions are not matters of reality; they are no more than conventional decisions concerning the use of certain linguistic expressions. If we change the definitions of "circle" and "square" then it may be possible for the same figure to be a square and also a circle. Definitions can be changed. Of course if we change the definitions of words whose definitions have become familiar, we create a lot of inconvenience, possible confusion; but it can be done. When we change the definitions of linguistic expressions we do not affect reality; we affect only language.

What is physical or practical impossibility? It has to do with matters of fact. Suppose I tell you that I can lift a house with my bare hands. Will you believe that? Of course not.

You will say, "Impossible." Now here the impossibility is physical, not logical. It is logically possible for me to lift a whole house with my bare hands, but it is physically impossible. The impossibility of my lifting a house with my bare hands is due to my lack of strength. Normally, a human being does not have enough strength to lift a whole house with his bare hands. But it is not logically impossible—we can think it. What can be thought is logically possible. There are many things that are logically possible which are not practically possible. A very good illustration is the landing of a human being on the moon. If you told people in 1900 that one day a man would plant a flag on the moon, they would have laughed at you. But even then it was not logically impossible; it was practically impossible in that at that time there was no technology to make it happen. But what was practically impossible in 1900 did happen in the 1970's: on TV we saw a man on the moon!

We return to Flew. Since Flew is a careful thinker let us not toy with the idea that he has made a naive mistake in reasoning. Rather let us ask ourselves why he would say what he says. Why would Flew be talking about logical impossibility when he is talking about experience and God, which are matters of reality and not of logic? There must be a reason. And there is. I believe the reason is that behind this argument of Flew is his assumption of the empiricist criterion of meaning and knowledge. In Chapter 1 we talked about the significance of assumptions; we said that assumptions are usually not stated but they are there. If one reads Flew's book, one gets the clear impression that he assumes the empiricist criterion. Flew does not admit that he does. But it is clear that he does. Now, given the assumption of the empiricist criterion of meaning and knowledge, then of course it is logically impossible to know that an experience is in any way related to God. According to the empiricist criterion of meaning and knowledge, a word or a sentence is meaningful if and only if it can be tested, verified, checked by means of the techniques of science. But the techniques of science cannot yield any data about God simply because God is Spirit, whereas the techniques of science can deal only with what can be observed. What cannot be seen, heard, tasted, touched, smelled cannot be tested by the techniques of science. And God cannot be seen, heard, tasted, touched, smelled. If God exists, science cannot know that fact. You cannot by the use of scientific instruments produce any data pointing to the existence of God. That is why as far as the empiricist is concerned, the word "God" and all other words related to the word "God" are meaningless. Science cannot make sense of God. Science cannot make sense of God-related experience. To the empiricist talk about God or God-related experience is nonsense. That is why Flew says it is logically impossible for any experience to guarantee that it is related to God. Experiences are psychological phenomena; they are matters of fact. But Flew's point is that there is nothing in any experience that can tell us that the experience is related to God. And when Flew says there is nothing he means there is nothing that can be verified by means of the techniques of science—there is nothing that passes the test of the empiricist criterion of meaning. Small wonder that Flew keeps using the word "necessarily" in the passage we have quoted. The word "necessarily" belongs to the domain of logic. For Flew, it is logically impossible to conclude to God from the character of any experience.

So what is our conclusion on Flew's objection? Our conclusion is that if the empiricist criterion of meaning and knowledge is adopted even when it is God we are talking about, then Flew's objection holds and does so beautifully. But if we reject the universal application of the empiricist criterion of meaning and knowledge, then Flew's objection is crippled. So the issue turns into the question of whether the empiricist criterion of meaning and knowledge must apply universally. The question is whether talk about God must be subjected to the empiricist razor. Why must the empiricist criterion apply universally? That is our two-hundred dollar question! We agree that when it comes to things that are amenable to sense observation the techniques of science are the best that we know. But why must we apply the techniques of science of all subject matters? There is nothing in science or in logic or in any other discipline that makes it mandatory that all people, including Christians, adopt the universal application of the empiricist criterion of meaning and knowledge.

6.2 REPLY TO GORDON STEIN, JOSEPH LEWIS, ROBERT INGERSOLL

Let us respond to other unbelievers on the subject of the Bible. Space does not allow us to reply to every point made by the selected unbelievers; neither obviously do we have space to respond to all unbelievers who have criticized the Bible or belief in the Bible. A thorough reply job requires several volumes just on the subject of the Bible.

First, let us reply to the atheist Gordon Stein. Dr. Stein is the editor of the 1985 two-volume Encyclopedia of Unbelief. he is also the editor of American Rationalist and associate editor of Free Inquiry. Stein has published several books in the area of unbelief. He is the author of several of the articles in The Encyclopedia of Unbelief. One of the articles is titled "Unbelief in Revelation." It is this article that we want to respond to now.

On p. 556, Vol. 2 of Encyclopedia of Unbelief Dr. Stein writes: "What is now called fundamentalism was called enthusiasm in the 18th century, a term meaning 'fanatic.' It survives today only among people of narrow educational background or persons who could be characterized as authoritarian personalities. Belief in literal revelation has tended to disappear among the great majority of Western Christians, both Protestant and Catholics, and survives only among the most orthodox Jews." (Emphasis added) There are three things in this passage from Gordon Stein that we want to comment on. Read again the first sentence of the passage we have quoted. Is Stein suggesting that "fundamentalism" = "fanatic"? Is it fair to read him as making that suggestion? If Stein is at least suggesting that fundamentalism = fanaticism, our response is this. The word "fundamentalist" happens nowadays to be an over-used noun. You hear the word "fundamentalist" so very often nowadays. Some people who apparently look down on fundamentalists have even coined a shorter form of the word: "fundy" (plural" "fundies"). A number of times I have heard people utter the word "fundies." Each time the person uttering the word laughed and some of the ones listening also laughed, which made me conclude that the user of the word meant the word to be used as a put-down. In the press conference after his reelection to the presidency of the Southern Baptist Convention in June 1987, Dr. Adrian Rogers was asked about his theological position. He said he objected to being called a fundamentalist because, to quote him, the word is 'more or less a pejorative term.' "I don't like to answer to that name," Rogers said. He said he preferred to be called a conservative.[20]   Rogers is right; many people nowadays use the term "fundamentalist" pejoratively. It is extremely important for one who uses the word to make clear what he means by it. The reader is reminded of what we said in Chapter 1, about the importance of making things clear. In the case of Stein's use of the word "fundamentalism" in the passage we have quoted we ask what Stein means by the word. Is he equating it with "fanatic"? It looks like he is. Now if he is, I am sure many people who classify themselves as fundamentalists, or who are usually classified by others as fundamentalists, will object to the equation fundamentalist = fanatic. Sometimes the word "fundamentalist" is used to refer to theologians or other people who defend the inerrancy of the Bible. Now there are today many such theologians. When we consider the fact that many theologians today are classified as fundamentalists because they believe in Biblical inerrancy, we cannot help wondering if Dr. Stein would apply his use of "Fundamentalist" (as meaning "fanatic") to these theologians. Does Stein mean to apply the put-down word "fanatic" to inerrantist theologians? We want to ask Stein: Is "fanatic" essentially involved in "fundamentalist"? That is, is every fundamentalist necessarily a fanatic? Are inerrantist theologians necessarily fanatics? Would Stein say that? It seems that one use of "fanatic" is to indicate the attitude of a person whose mind is closed. A fanatic is one who is unreasonable, excessively enthusiastic and zealous, one who is governed more by emotion than reason, one whose thinking is not too reliable.

The trouble with the word "fanatic" is that it has a highly negative ring to it. For some people the word "fanatic" is emotively charged.

Let us focus now on the second sentence of the passage we have quoted. Stein says, "It [fundamentalism] survives today [1985, when The Encyclopedia of Unbelief was published] only among people of narrow educational background or persons who could be characterized as authoritarian personalities." Let us take the first part of the sentence first. Stein says fundamentalism survives ONLY among people of narrow educational background (emphasis mine). Is that true? Are all who are willing to be called fundamentalist when it comes to the interpretation of the Bible—are they all of narrow educational background? What does Stein mean by "narrow educational background"? Does he mean "little education"? If that is what he means, he is clearly wrong. In the current debate on the issue of Biblical inerrancy, one finds many articles and books in favor of Biblical inerrancy which are written by people with earned doctor's degrees.

Part of our problem in responding to this sentence of Stein is that he has not made his meaning very clear. As I run in my mind through the names of authors whom Stein would very likely classify as fundamentalist, I see that many of them have credentials that cannot be called narrow in the sense of little. Take the case of John W. Montgomery, one of the writers who defend Biblical inerrancy. Montgomery has earned two doctorate degrees and has written a number of books. He obtained his undergraduate degree in classics with honors from Cornell University. Is that little educational background? Take Gleason Archer, another believer in Biblical inerrancy. He had a law degree and a Ph.D. in theology. Is that narrow educational background? Take Carl F. H. Henry; he has a Ph.D. in theology and a Ph.D. in philosophy. I read the names of the faculty of a conservative seminary. All their professors had doctorates; several had two Ph.D.s. Among evangelical theologians who believe in Biblical inerrancy the educational credentials are impressive.

Or does "narrow" as used by Stein mean "specialized"? Nowadays narrow in the sense of specialized is normal; because of the knowledge explosion, doctoral studies tend to be specialized.

The second part of the sentence we are dealing with is interesting. Stein says fundamentalism survives today only among people with narrow educational backgrounds "or persons who could be characterized as authoritarian personalities." What does he mean by the second half of this sentence? He is saying (isn't he?) that if one is a fundamentalist then if he is not a person with narrow educational background then he is an authoritarian personality—or possibly both. Whom does Stein call an authoritarian personality? Later in this same article, on p. 557, we have some clarification. Writes Stein: "Most fundamentalists, however, are unreflective and, as mentioned, fit the pattern of the 'authoritarian personality.' Here we get what Stein means by "authoritarian personality"; he is a person who is unreflective, unthinking. Most fundamentalists, Stein says, are unreflective; they are authoritarian personalities. Most fundamentalists are unreflective, authoritarian persons? This is not only quite false but also quite unfair. As we have said it is very probable that Stein would classify as fundamentalist those evangelical theologians who believe in Biblical inerrancy. In that case Stein is saying that most Bible inerrantists are unreflective, unthinking, persons. Has Stein seriously read the articles and books written by Bible inerrantists with respectable educational credentials? I wonder. Before anyone can be in a position to say that most fundamentalists are unreflective, he should have read most if not all the writings of fundamentalist authors. And there are many such authors. If one has not read their writings, then he is not in a position to pass any judgments such as that most fundamentalists are unreflective.

This false and unscholarly judgment only makes us wonder if Stein is not guilty of talking out of a high level of prejudice. Is a theologian unreflective, unthinking simply because in his study he reaches the conclusion that the Bible is inerrant? Is it only the liberals, the rationalists, the neo-orthodox thinkers who know how to think? Such a judgment is not only ungenerous, unscholarly; it is also quite false.

The main trouble with resorting to name-calling and similar strategies is that the discussion is shifted from issues to personalities. Argumentum ad hominem (argument directed to the man instead of the issues) is fallacious. It is particularly unfortunate if those who indulge in name-calling and put-down adjectives do not take the trouble to seriously read the writings of those they so confidently evaluate negatively.

Still on p. 557, Stein writes: "Thus, in this highly individualistic form of Protestantism, at one time much favored among Southern Baptists and other conservative sects, revelation is first and foremost personal experience." Stein classifies Southern Baptists as a sect. Is he using the word "sect" properly? According to Webster's New Twentieth Century Dictionary, a sect is a " religious denomination, especially a small group that has broken away from an established church." Surely, the Southern Baptist denomination is not a small group. A denomination that is one of the fastest growing in the United States and that now counts thousands of congregations all over the United States and overseas—is that a small group? The August 17, 1987 issue of Christianity Today describes the Southern Baptist group as "the nation's largest Protestant denomination" (p.37).

Stein says that in what he calls fundamentalist Protestantism, as represented by Southern Baptists, "revelation is first and foremost personal experience." This is very wrong. Many Christians who count themselves as conservative theologically will vehemently object to that view of Gordon Stein. For them revelation is absolutely not "first and foremost" personal experience. It is not even that in a secondary sense. For conservatives, revelation is God's making Himself known to the world in and through the prophets and apostles and primarily in and through Jesus Christ. The prophets' refrain was, "Thus saith the Lord." It was not their experience they were talking about; it was God's message that the prophets were communicating. "Thus SAITH the Lord." There may be some isolated conservative individuals who think of revelation primarily in terms of personal experience. But that is definitely not the line taken by Southern Baptists or other conservative groups. I really wonder if Stein has read the articles and books written by conservatives in theology. He specifically mentions the Southern Baptists as representative of what he calls fundamentalism. If he has read the doctrinal statement of the Southern Baptist denomination he would not be able to make the claim that for Southern Baptists revelation is first and foremost personal experience. In my own reading I have not yet come across a single conservative theologian who thinks revelation first and foremost in terms of personal experience. Individual Christians have their personal God-related experiences, yes, but no conservative theologian that I have read thinks that such personal experiences is the essence of revelation. Revelation is always thought of first and foremost in terms of the events and teachings recorded in the Bible.

Still on p. 557 Stein writes: "Among fundamentalists, in effect, the divinely revealed authority is actually the preacher or elder who interprets scripture rather than scripture itself— or the community of believers in more democratic situations—so that . . . consensus is the real authority. The divinely revealed word is not scripture alone or even primarily but rather what is held to be the will of God in the particular community." Here is another grossly mistaken assertion. Fundamentalist authors speak of authority always in terms of Scripture. It is true that there is a discipline called hermeneutics, the discipline of interpretation. But interpretation is not the authority or the source of authority. Conservative theologians always talk in terms of the authority of the written Word of God, never in terms of the preacher or the exegete. Exegesis is not at all the seat of authority as far as conservative theologians are concerned. I have not yet come across any conservative Bible commentator who gave the reader the slightest impression that <u>his</u> commentary was the source or seat of authority. Conservative interpreters of the Bible rely on the guidance of the Holy Spirit as they seek to understand the written Word of God. But always authority is taken to lie in the written Word of God—not in any interpreter or preacher. Dr. Stein should listen to conservative preachers so he will know where the preacher places authority. In all the years of listening to conservative preachers, I have not yet heard one preacher who arrogated authority unto himself or his interpretation of the passage he was preaching from. Always the appeal is to the authority of the written word of God. One wonders if Dr. Stein has ever heard a conservative preacher preaching.

On p. 558 Stein writes: "Officially or not, the authority of revelation rests with consensus . . . ." Perhaps what Stein has in mind here is the formation of the canon, that is, the list of books that now compose the Old and the New Testaments. Stein is saying here, I take it, that the authority of revelation lies in the canon, or in the church bodies that determined which books were to be admitted into the canon. In reply, let us advert to the point we have made earlier. The writings that were admitted into the canon were so admitted because they were deemed to be authoritative, i.e., because they were believed to have been written under the inspiration of God. The truth is that both logically and historically authority precedes canonicity—not the other way around. Stein reverses the truth here. The authority of revelation does not lie in the church bodies that came to the agreement that such and such writings were divinely inspired. The authority of Scripture, or revelation, lies in the writings themselves, in their having been written under divine inspiration.

It is important to note that in this article, in which he rejects revelation, Stein does not say even one word about the role of the Holy Spirit in the writing of the Bible books. This fact is very significant. To the Christian, the role of the Holy Spirit is extremely important, both in the writing of the books that now compose the Bible and also in the determination of the writings that were admitted into the canon. The role of the

Holy Spirit in the on going work of interpreting Scripture is also very important. But Stein does not believe in the Holy Spirit since he rejects the supernatural. He starts with his atheist assumptions; so whatever he says in commenting about theology or theologians will logically exclude any role of God.

I find it also remarkable that in Stein's critique of fundamentalism in this article he does not give examples; he does not quote passages from the writings of fundamentalist theologians to substantiate his assertions. It would have been easier to see what he bases his assertions on. As it is, we are left guessing if he has read any conservative theologian's writings or if he is just working from the a high degree of prejudice.

Now let us turn to a comment on the Bible by the president of Freethinkers of America, the atheist Joseph Lewis. In a TV interview in 1957, Lewis said:[21]

The Bible is a fraud because: first, every historian of any repute has condemned it for interfering with intellectual progress. Almost every science that we're acquainted with has condemned it because it interferes with the progress of that particular science and their particular researches. All we have to do is to take, for instance, the story of Galileo . . . . Take the story of Bruno. Bruno, a great scientist of his day, was burned at the stake in 1600 by the Church because he promulgated doctrines that were contrary to the church's teachings. . . . . Even Copernicus was so concerned for his life, his great scientific discovery was not published in his lifetime, for fear of being burnt at the stake. . . . . So great was the fear of the Church, at that time, that even the great Leonardo de Vinci wrote many of his scientific articles in a disguise handwriting. So great was the Church's power during the Middle Ages that dissection was prohibited and even anaesthesia was condemned as contrary to God's will.

Lewis says the Bible is a fraud because "every historian of any repute has condemned it for interfering with intellectual progress." This assertion is simply false. We do not deny that some historians have attacked the Bible. But to say that every historian of any repute has condemned the Bible is clearly an unwarranted exaggeration; it is clearly false. Normally a theological seminary has at least one professor teaching church history. And normally such people have a doctorate degree in history in addition to their theological degrees. Many of such professors have written books. My professor in church history at the seminary had a D. Phil. and had published a number of books. At seminary I had a classmate who had a Ph.D. in history and who had been a professor of history a good number of years. She was preparing for the Christian ministry.

Lewis implies that historians who do not condemn the Bible are of no repute. What is Lewis' criterion for determining that a given historian has repute? That is a very interesting question. Many times in debate a debater resorts to ad hominems, to attacking personalities instead of addressing themselves to issues. The attack sometimes takes the form of saying that those who disagree are of no repute or something to that affect. Lewis would say, I take it, that if a historian believes the Bible, that historian does not count, he is fourth or fifth rate. It is those historians who condemn the Bible who are great as far as Lewis is concerned. Reputable historians will not buy that criterion.

Lewis mentions the cases of Galileo, Bruno, Copernicus. We agree that the cases of Galileo, Bruno, and all others who were persecuted by the church because of their scientific activities are a black mark in the history of the church. The history of the church records many condemnable acts perpetrated by the church. Many church leaders have done quite unchristian things. Church historians are the first to say that. That we do not deny. From the very early days of Christianity there have been believers who did not seriously live by the teachings in the Bible. But the church is not the Bible. The integrity of the Bible is not measured by the lives of those who profess to believe the Bible. We must distinguish the behavior of those who profess to be Christians from the Bible. The Bible is the written word of God. Its truth is <u>independent</u> of the behavior of those who profess to believe the Bible. But the fact that there are backsliding Bible believers does not alter the truth of what the Bible says; it does not diminish the Bible's authority.

Perhaps some parallel can be drawn with laws passed by legislatures. Legislatures continue to pass laws and presidents continue to sign the bills passed by the legislatures. But all the time there are many people who violate existing laws. There are good laws which are not kept by all the citizens of the land; there are always violators of the law; some of them are apprehended, some are not. But the fact that there are many violators of existing laws does not diminish the wisdom or authority of those laws. The fact that some people violate a given law does not make that law bad; if it is a good law, it is a good law, no matter how many violators of it there are. Its goodness is inherent in itself. Whether people obey a given law or not is external to the law; it does not determine the law's quality or authority.

There are many who profess to be followers of Jesus Christ whose lives say something else. That does not make Jesus Christ any less the Son of God and the only Savior.

In saying this we are of course not advocating easy believism—far from it. (In Chapter 5 we discussed discipleship at some length in connection with John 8:31-32; so we will not develop this matter here. The reader is referred to Chapter 5.)

In the same TV interview, Lewis said, "There may have been people who, out of pure hypocrisy, have praised the Bible for its moral values. And yet it does not contain a moral guide." This claim of Lewis is so wrong that we feel it does not merit a serious reply. Anyone who has read the Bible knows the ethical aspects of the Bible's teachings.

Lewis says those who praise the moral values of the Bible do so "out of pure hypocrisy." Remarks like this bring the discussion down to a less than serious level.

Let us turn now to Robert Ingersoll's view about the inspiration of the Scriptures. Ingersoll is considered by some as the greatest 19th century unbeliever in the United States. One of the lectures reprinted in the book Ingersoll's Greatest Lectures (1944) is titled "Inspiration." Here the great agnostic gives us his view of the doctrine of inspiration.

Ingersoll says: "What is meant by the word 'inspired' is not exactly known; but whatever else it may mean, certainly it means that the word 'inspired' must be the truth. If it is true, there is in fact no need of its being inspired-the truth will take care of itself." The first thing we notice here is Ingersoll's assertion that the meaning of "inspired" (as applied to the Bible) is not exactly known. What does he mean by that? He and other unbelievers may not know the meaning of "inspired"; but Christians do; at least many Christians do. We know that to say that the Scriptures are the inspired word of God means that the men who wrote the Scriptures were guided by the Spirit of God. In the second letter of the apostle Peter we read: "First of all you must understand this, that no prophecy of scripture is a matter of one's own interpretation, because no prophecy ever came by the impulse of man, but men moved by the Holy Spirit spoke from God" (II Peter 1:20-21). That's what the doctrine of inspiration means, that the men who wrote what is now the Bible did not write their own ideas; moved by the Holy Spirit they wrote God's message. What they wrote was not the result of their own research or investigation; they wrote as they were moved by the Spirit of God. That is why Christians speak of the Bible as the written word of God. The prophets characteristically prefaced their proclamation with "Thus saith the Lord."

Continuing from the sentence quoted above, Ingersoll says: "If it [i.e., the inspired word] is true, there is in fact no need of its being inspired—the truth will take care of itself." This statement is the result of Ingersoll's ignorance of the meaning of "inspired." The word of God is true, yes, but it was not inspired in order that it would become true. Inspiration has to do with the communication of God's word; it does not refer to the truth of the word of God. Whether communicated or not, the word of God is true; its being true does not derive from its being communicated through the men moved by the Holy Spirit to communicate it; its truth lies in its being the word of God.

The main point made by Ingersoll in this lecture is that what we understand of the Scriptures depends on us—on our background, our abilities, our experience, and so on. Ingersoll offers several illustrations all trying to show that what we get from a book or a painting or a flower or the sea or anything else is what we are capable of getting or inclined to get. "So, when we look upon a flower, a painting, a statue, a star, or a violet, the more we know, the more we have experienced, the more we have thought, the more we remember—the more the statue, the star, the painting, the violet, has to tell. Nature says to me all that I am capable of understanding—given all that I can receive" (p.385). Then he gives the reader his punch line: "The supernatural can be constructed with no material except the natural. Of the supernatural we can have no conception." The point he has been hammering with his several illustrations is that what we get from anything, what we can understand, depends on what we are or have, on what we bring to the thing. So a man's idea of God and God's will or God's message is nothing but a "construction" from what humans contribute. But man is natural and can only contribute what is natural. Man does not understand anything of the supernatural—he only thinks he does. "Above the natural, man cannot rise." "Some people have ideas about what they are pleased to call the supernatural; what they call the supernatural is simply the deformed. The world is to each man according to each man." "As with everything in Nature, so with the Bible. It has a different story for each reader. Is then, the Bible a different book to every human being who reads it? It is. Can God, then, through the Bible, make the same revelation to two persons? He cannot. Why? Because the man who reads it is the man who inspires. Inspiration is in the man, as well as in the book. God should have 'inspired' readers as well as writers" (p. 386). Let us examine this passage. Ingersoll asserts that of the supernatural man can have no idea at all. If he, Ingersoll, had no idea of the supernatural at all, it does not follow that Christians are as ignorant as he. He should not speak for all men; Ingersoll should speak only for himself and his fellow unbelievers. Christians do have a definite conception of the supernatural; God has revealed Himself enough for believers to have a good working conception of the supernatural. The way to have an idea of the supernatural is to read the Bible.

Ingersoll says the Bible is "a different book to every human being who reads it." In other words, each reader of the Bible understands of it something different from what any other man understands. One is tempted to say that assessments like this do not deserve to be taken seriously. Whoever reads the Bible with an open mind will see that so very much of the Bible is so clear and definite in its meaning that any two or more persons will not disagree as to what the passage is saying—provided of course they all understand the original language or the language into which the Bible has been translated. Of course there are passages that are not so easy to understand, passages which two or more readers could interpret differently; that is not denied. But for the most part, the Bible is clear and definite in its meaning. One does not have to have a college degree to understand the Bible. But of course if one has already made up his mind that the Bible is so dense that no two persons can get the same sense from any given passage—well, what can we say to that? The best thing to say is, "Read it." (I might say again here that when I was 31 years old, after some six years of calling myself a freethinker, it was my reading the Bible for one year that led me to receiving Jesus Christ as my personal Savior and Lord. If Ingersoll and company would say I did not understand what I read—I fold up my hands.)

Ingersoll ends this lecture with this sentence: "The inspiration of the Bible depends upon the ignorance of him who reads" (p.387). Again it's Ingersoll's idea that each man is the measure of everything, including the Bible.

To close our response to Ingersoll on the subject of inspiration, let us examine the logic of his position. Ingersoll's key idea in this lecture is that each man is the measure of everything. Each man gets what he can from a book or a painting or something else according to what he brings into it. Since no two persons have the same abilities, experiences, beliefs, interests, likes and dislikes, etc., therefore it is quite unlikely that two persons reading the same book come out with the same understanding of what the book is saying. Now if Ingersoll is right, then what happens to truth? It makes no sense to speak of truth. No man can say what he thinks or says is true—and no man is in the position to say yes or no to anyone's claim that what he says is true. In that case, why did Ingersoll waste his time giving a lecture on inspiration? How did he expect people to learn from him or to believe what he said? What did he expect them to get from his lectures? On what basis did Ingersoll expect anyone to agree with him? And if there was no basis for any of his listeners or readers to agree—or disagree—with him, what was the point of saying anything at all?

6.3. ON THE LITERAL INTERPRETATION OF THE BIBLE

We cannot emphasize enough the need of clarity. We often encounter words whose meanings are unclear and yet those who use them apparently think that their meaning is clear. In the hurry of conversation or even in writing, we all too often do not take the time to make our meanings clear; we often assume that the words we are using are understood by others in exactly the way we intend them to be understood. Unfortunately that is sometimes not the case. So whatever the subject of our talk, we need to endeavor to make our intended meaning clear.

One word that in my observation is problematic is the word "literal" when applied to interpreting the Bible. What does it mean to interpret the Bible literally?

Before we address that question directly, let us distinguish "sentence" and "proposition" (or "statement"). As we learned in the grades, a sentence is a group of words used to express a thought. The joining of words together to form a sentence

is governed by certain rules (of grammar). Now the group of
words (i. e., the sentence) is different from the thought, or idea,
or sense that it expresses. It is because sentences are different
from the ideas, or thoughts, or senses that they express, that it
is possible to translate a sentence in one language into another
language without changing the idea expressed. In the same
language, we can express the same idea in different words: "2
is less than 4" says the same thing as "4 is greater than 2."

What we are calling "proposition" (or "statement") is the
idea, or thought, or sense that the sentence expresses. Strictly,
a sentence cannot be true or false. What is true—or false—is
the proposition, not the sentence, The proposition is true—or
false—depending on the state of affairs that the proposition
refers to. Suppose there is a black cat on the bench and
suppose we say, "There is a white cat on the bench." When we
hear the sentence "There is a white cat on the bench" we expect
to see a cat which is white. We look and we see a black cat on
the bench. The state of affairs does not agree with the sense
expressed by the sentence we have heard. So we say the
statement is false—or we say the sentence we have heard
expresses a false statement. To determine truth or falsity we
need to check the state of affairs denoted by the statement
expressed by the sentence. So there are three things that must
be distinguished: the sentence, the proposition (or statement),
and the state of affairs. A statement (or proposition) is true if
what it says is so.

Now let us refer to the subject of interpreting the Bible.
What does it mean to speak of interpreting a Bible passage
literally? Does it mean to take the words as they stand in their
normal, usual sense regardless of the genre (type of literature)
of the passage? Or does literal interpretation allow for treating
poetry differently from prose? In literal interpretation, are
figures of speech treated as figures of speech? Perhaps my
point might be made clear if I ask the question this way: In
literal interpretation of a Bible passage, are we committed to
taking each word as it stands regardless of how it functions in
the sentence, regardless of the genre to which the passage
belongs? Or are we governed by the distinction between

sentence and proposition?

To make my point clear, let us take a specific passage. Take as our example Psalm 23. Ps. 23:1 reads: "The Lord is my shepherd...." If we take the word "shepherd" alone, what does it point us to? Does it point us to God? No; it points us to a human being, usually a male person, who tends sheep or goats. We normally associate shepherd and cane. When we hear the word "shepherd" we have in mind a man walking in front of a flock of sheep. That is the normal—the usual—use of the word "shepherd." Now if literal interpretation is taken to mean taking each word in the sentence in its normal, or usual sense in prose, then part of what "The Lord is my shepherd" says is that God is a shepherd, that is, God is a human being that tends sheep. Which of course is absurd.

It is different if we ask what proposition "The Lord is my shepherd" expresses. Now we are not tied strictly to the usual, or normal, use of each word in the sentence. When we ask what proposition is expressed by the sentence, we are forced to consider the genre to which the sentence belongs, that is, we have to consider what type of literature the passage is. Is it prose? Is it poetry? Is it a figure of speech? What figure of speech is it? In a figure of speech we do not take the individual words in their normal use; we take the entire sentence and ask what proposition it expresses. Taken as a figure of speech— taken in terms of its proper genre—"The Lord is my shepherd" says something like "The Lord takes care of me," or "The Lord protects me." What is stated is the relationship that normally obtains between shepherd and the sheep under his care. You will notice that if we keep in mind the distinction between sentence and proposition, and if we take into account the genre of the passage we are interpreting, we avoid absurd interpretations.

Let us take one more example. Take Psalm 23:4: "Even though I walk through the valley of the shadow of death, I fear no evil...." If we take each word in this sentence in its usual use, then we find ourselves puzzling over the question of what the shadow of death is. Does death have a shadow? Does that make sense? If we take each word in the sentence in its normal use, this sentence does not say anything to us since we cannot make sense of "shadow of death." That is as meaningless as "last night I had a 75- foot-tall dream that smelled like twenty kilometers."

Some people talk as if conservative Christians interpret every Bible passage literally in the sense of always taking every word in every sentence in its natural, usual sense, ignoring such things as figures of speech. Are there Christians who read the Bible that way? I ask that question because I find it very hard to believe that there are Christians who read Ps. 23:1 (for example) as saying, among other things, that God is a human being, a shepherd. I doubt very much if there are Christians who read the Bible like that. I think even conservatives read figures of speech as figures of speech.

The advantage of distinguishing sentence and proposition is that proposition is not affected by genre. Sentence is. The proposition intended by "The Lord is my shepherd" is not "The Lord is a human being who tends sheep and he has that relationship to me"; the first clause of this sentence expresses a false idea since God is not a human being. In interpreting a passage, the first important question we must ask is: What type of literature is this? In interpreting the Bible we abide by the norms of interpretation we learned in English classes in high school and college.

EPILOGUE

The curtain has fallen. As we bring this thinking together to a close, three things I want to say. First, I must acknowledge the probability that the reader feels that we have covered so little ground. I share that feeling. There are so many assertions/arguments of unbelievers we have not touched. Unbelievers are continuing to write in opposition to Christian belief. Already so much has been published by them.

Secondly: If I have succeeded in making the Christian community more aware of the challenge from unbelievers, then much of what I hoped to accomplish in this effort would have been realized.

Thirdly: I hope to see more books produced by Christians addressing the challenge posed by unbelief.

This Christian his little candle; that Christian his little lamp, yonder Christian his little torch. In the hands of God, the little lights can provide the world a sustained testimony that the camp of Jesus Christ is here to stay. And the greatest fact of all is that that hope is built on the tremendous fact that the Spirit of God is still working in the world.

God is watching over His word!

NOTES

CHAPTER ZERO   MY FINDING THE WAY
   1. B. A. G. Fuller and Steling McMurrin, <u>A History of Philosophy</u>, 3rd ed., Pt. II (New York: Henry Holt and Company.

CHAPTER ONE   SOME PRELIMINARY MATTERS
   1. Arthur Howland, <u>Joseph Lewis, Enemy of God</u> (Boston: Stratford Co., 1032), p. 18.
   2. Joseph Lewis, <u>Atheism and Other Addresses</u> (New York: Freethought Press Assn, 1960), page not indicated.
   3. Robert Ingersoll, <u>Ingersoll's Greatest Lectures</u> (New York: Freethought Press Assn., 1944), p. 431.
   4. Alfred Ayer, <u>Language, Truth and Logic</u> (New York: Dover Publications, Inc.,_____), p. 11.
   5. <u>Ibid.</u>, p. 115.
   6. Arthur Pap, <u>Elements of Analytic Philosophy</u> (New York: The Macmillan Comapny, 1949), p. 477.
   7. Edward Young, cited by R. C. Sproul, "The Case for Inerrancy : A Methodological Analysis," in <u>God's Inerrant Word</u>, ed. John W. Montgomery (Minneapolis: Bethany Fellowship, Inc., 1974), p. 258.

CHAPTER TWO SCIENCE AND CHRISTIAN FAITH
   1. Albert Van der Ziel, <u>The Natural Sciences and the Christian Message</u> (Minneapolis: Dennison, 1960), p. 14.
   2. Bertrand Russell, <u>Religion and Science</u> (New York:

Henry Holt & Co., 1935), p. 8.

    3. Isaac Asimov, "The Scientist as Unbeliever," in The Encyclopedia of Unbelief, vol. 2, p. 611.

    4. David Brooks, M.D., The Necessity of Atheism (New York: Freethought Press Assn., 1933), p. 122.

    5. Tad Clements, Science and Man(Springfield: Clark Thomas, Pub., 1968) p. 27.

CHAPTER THREE   MIRACLES

    1. A. Wolf, Essentials of Scientific Method (London: Allen and Unwin, 1925), p. 124.

    2. Isaac Asimov, "The Scientist ans Unbeliever," in The Encyclopedia of Unbelief ed. Gordon Stein, vol. 2 (Buffalo: Prometheus Books, 1985), p. 611.

    3. A. Wolf, Essentials of Scientific Method, p. 112.

    4. Ibid., p. 103.

CHAPTER FIVE   CHRISTIAN FAITH

    1. Quoted in David Brooks, M.D., The Necessity of Atheism (New York: Freethought Press Assn., 1933), p. 309.

    2. Cyril E. M. Joad, The Recovery of Belief (London: Faber & Faber, 1952), p. 18.

CHAPTER SIX   THE BIBLE

    1. Martin Kahler, The So-Called Historical Jesus and the Biblical Christ trans. Carl Braaten, 1964, p. 75; cited by R. C. Sproul in "The Case for Inerrancy: A Methodological Analysis," in God's Inerrant Word ed. John W. Montgomery (Minneapolis: Bethany Fellowship, Inc., 1974), p. 257.

    2. A. Berkeley Mickelsen, Interpreting the Bible (Grand Rapids: Eerdmans, 1963), pp. 80-84.

    3. Eusebius Pamphilus, Ecclesiastical History, trans. C. F. Cruse (Philadelphia: J. P. Lippincott & Co., 1860), p. 127.

    4. F. F. Bruce, Are the New Testament Documents Reliable? (Grand Rapids: Eerdmans, 1954), pp. 18-19.

    5. Ibid., pp. vii-viii.

    6. Ibid., p. 19.

7. Sir Frederick Kenyon, Handbook to the Textual Criticism of the New Trestament, 2nd ed. (Longon: Macmillan, 1912), p. 5; cited by John W. Montgomery, History and Christianity (Downer's Grove: Inter Varisty Press, 1964), pp. 26-27.

8. John W. Montgomery, History and Christianity, p. 28.

9. Sir Frederick Kenyon, The Bible and Archaeology (New York: Harper, 1940), pp. 288-89: cited by John W. Montgomery, History and Christianity, p. 28.

10. E. M. Blaiklock, Archaeology of the New Testament, rev. ed. (Nashville: Thomas Nelson, 1984), p. 1.

11. Ibid., pp. 1-2.

12. James Prichard, Archaeology and the Old Testament, (Princeton: Princeton University Press, 1958), pp. 246-47.

13. Sir William Ramsay, The Bearing of Recent Discovery on the Trustworthiness of the New Testament(reprint) (Grand Rapids: Baker Book House, 1952), p. 81; cited by John W. Montgomery in History and Christianity, pp. 31-32.

14. Keith Schoville, Biblical Archaeology in Focus (Grand Rapids: Baker Book House, 1978), p. 447.

15. William Brownlee, The Meaning of the Qumran Scrolls for the Bible (New York: Oxford Univ. Press, 1964), p. 3.

16. F. F. Bruce, Second Thoughts on the Dead Sea Scrolls (Grand Rapids: Eerdmans, 1956), p. 59.

17. Ibid., p. 69.

18. Roland K. Harrison, "Bible," in The International Standard Bible Encyclopedia vol. 1, G. W. Bromily, gen. ed. (Grand Rapids: Eerdmans, 1979), p. 491.

19. Antony Flew, God and Philosophy (New York: Dell Publishing Co., 1966), pp. 131-132.

20. Baptist Standard, June 24, 1987, p. 5.

21. Joseph Lewis, Atheism and Other Addresses(New York: Freethought Press Assn., 1960), pages not given; no chapter numbers given either. The passage quoted is found in the address titled "Lou Gordon Interviews Lewis on TV."

SOURCES CONSULTED

Archer, Gleason. "The Witness of the Bible to Its Own
   Inerrancy." In The Foundations of Biblical
   Authority, ed. James Boice. Grand Rapids:
   Zondervan, 1978.
Ayer, Alfred, ed. Logical Positivism. New York: The
   Free Press, 1959.
Blaiklock, E. M. The Archaeology of the New
   Testament rev. ed. Nashville: Thomas Nelson,
   1984.
Bromiley, G. W., gen. ed. The International Standard
   Bible Encyclopedia, vol. 1. Grand Rapids:
   Eerdmans, 1979.
Brooks, David. The Necessity of Atheism. New York:
   Freethought Press Assn., 1933.
Brownlee, William. The Meaning of the Qumran Scrolls
   for the Bible. New York: Oxford University Press,
   1964.
Bruce, F. F. The Books and the Parchments, rev. ed.
   Old Tappan: Fleming Revell Co., 1963.
   Second Thoughts on the Dead Sea Scrolls. Grand
   Rapids: Eerdmans, 1956.
Burns, R. M. The Great Debate on Miracles.
   Lewisburg: Bushnell University Press, 1981.
Clements, Tad. Science and Man. Springfield: Clark
   Thomas, 1968.
Flew, Antony. God and Philosophy. New York: Dell

167

Publishing Co., 1966.

Frame, John. "Scripture Speaks for Itself." In God's
Inerrant Word, ed. John W. Montgomery.
Minneapolis: Bethany Fellowship, Inc., 1973.

Fuller, B. A. and S. M. McMurrin. A History of
Philosophy, 3ed ed. New York: Henry Holt & Co.,
1955.

Grant, Frederick. The Earlest Gospel. New York:
Abingdon Cokesbury Press, 1943.

Harrison, R. K. Introduction to the Old Testament.
Grand Rapids: Eerdmans, 1969.

Henry, Carl F. H. God, Revelation and Authority, vol.
4. Waco: Word, 1979.

Howland, Arthur. Joseph Lewis, Enemy of God.
Boston: The Strafford Co., 1932.

Hume, David. An Enquiry Into Human Understanding,
2nd ed. LaSalle: Open Court, 1966.

Ingersoll, Robert. Ingersoll's Greatest Lectures. New
York: Freethought Press Assn., 1944.

Joad, Cyril E. M. The Recovery of Belief. London:
Faber and Faber, 1952.

Kantzer, Kenneth. "Evangelicals and the Doctrine of
Inerrancy." In The Foundations of Biblical
Authority, ed. James Boice. Grand Rapids:
Eerdmans, 1963.

Montgomery, John W. "Biblical Inerrancy: What Is at
Stake?" In God's Inerrant Word, ed. John W.
Montgomery. Minneapolis: Bethany Fellowship,
Inc., 1973.
History and Christianity. Downer's Grove: Inter-
Varsity Press, 1964.

Murray, John. "The Attestation of Scripture." In The
Infallible Word. Philadelphia: The Presbyterian
Guardian Pub. Corp., 1946.

Prichard, James. Archaeology and the Old Testament.
Princeton: Princeton University Press, 1958.

Pinnock, Clark. "The Inspiration of Scripture and the
Authority of Jesus Christ." In God's Inerrant Word,

ed. J. W. Montgomery.

Pamphilus, Eusebius. Ecclesiastical History. Trans. Christian Cruse. Philadelphia: J. P. Lippincott & Co., 1860.

Pap, Arthur. Elements of Analytic Philosophy. New York: Macmillan, 1949.

Ramm, Bernard. "Is 'Scripture Alone' the Essence of Christianity?" In Biblical Authority, ed. Jack Rogers. Waco: Word Books, 1977.

Schoville, Keith. Biblical Authority in Focus. Grand Rapids: Baker Book House, 1978.

Sproul, R. C. "The Case for Inerrancy: A Methodological Analysis." In God's Inerrant Word, ed. John W. Montgomery.

Stein, Bordon. "Unbelief in Revelation." In The Encyclopedia of Unbelief, ed. Gordon Stein. Buffalo: Prometheus Books, 1985.

Van der Ziel, Albert. The Natural Sciences and the Christian Message. Minneapolis: Dennison, 1960.

Van Til, Cornelius. A Christian Theory of Knowledge. Nutby: Presbyterian and Reformed Pub. Co., 1977.

Wolfe, A. Essentials of Scientific Method. London: Allen and Unwin, 1925.